TRACING YOUR FAMILY HISTORY ON THE INTERNET

FAMILY HISTORY FROM PEN & SWORD

TRACING YOUR FAMILY HISTORY ON THE INTERNET

A Guide for Family Historians

CHRIS PATON

Pen & Sword
FAMILY HISTORY

First published in Great Britain in 2011 by
PEN & SWORD FAMILY HISTORY
an imprint of
Pen & Sword Books Ltd
47 Church Street
Barnsley
South Yorkshire
S70 2AS

ISBN 978-1-84884-268-7

A CIP catalogue record for this book
is available from the British Library

Typeset in 10/12pt Palatino by
Concept, Huddersfield

Printed and bound in England by
CPI UK

Pen & Sword Books Ltd incorporates the Imprints of Pen & Sword
Aviation, Pen & Sword Maritime, Pen & Sword Military, Wharncliffe
Local History, Pen & Sword Select, Pen & Sword Military Classics,
Leo Cooper, Remember When, Seaforth Publishing and
Frontline Publishing.

For a complete list of Pen & Sword titles please contact
PEN & SWORD BOOKS LIMITED
47 Church Street, Barnsley, South Yorkshire, S70 2AS, England
E-mail: enquiries@pen-and-sword.co.uk
Website: www.pen-and-sword.co.uk

CONTENTS

GLOSSARY

BMD	Births, marriages and deaths
FHS	Family History Society
GEDCOM (.ged)	a file format, short for GEnealogical Data COMmunication – used to store and transfer information between different family tree software programmes
GRO	General Register Office
IGI	International Genealogical Index
MI	Monumental Inscription
NAS	National Archives of Scotland
NHS	National Health Service
OPC	Online Parish Clerk
OPR	Old Parochial Records – commonly used term to describe Scottish parish records
OS	Ordnance Survey
PCC wills	Prerogative Court of Canterbury wills
PDF (.pdf)	Portable Document Format – a data file format requiring an Adobe-based reader programme to access
Podcast	A digitally-based audio or video file which can be downloaded to your computer to view or listen to
PRONI	Public Record Office of Northern Ireland
TNA	The National Archives
URL	A website address – stands for 'Uniform Resource Locator'

PREFACE

The internet is the world's largest library, and used wisely can dramatically change our family history research for the better. The ease with which we can access material, however, can be seductive and sometimes dangerous if we do not remain in control of the research process and understand the nature of the records that we are consulting. As with offline resources, the key to successful research lies in maintaining rigorous standards when considering any potential documentary materials.

The internet is not just a vast repository of information. It also provides discussion forums within which we can pool our efforts with like-minded researchers, blogs and newsletters where we can obtain the latest information on new collections being released, family tree sites through which we can upload our pedigrees, and considerably more. The internet allows us to both look for information and to look for help.

This book is not about the etiquette of online research or the various technical considerations to be considered when using the internet. Nor is it a beginner's book to teach you how to research your family history, though it does provide some useful tips along the way. It largely assumes that you know the basics and that you wish to know where to look online to help find further resources for your research. It flags up the most useful sites for research within the United Kingdom, and explains what you are likely to find within them.

Regrettably, in producing this book I have on occasion had to substitute some website addresses with shortcuts. In particular, many government authorities seem to have a love affair with making their website addresses longer than the Chinese alphabet, a good example being the website for the National Library of Wales Family History catalogue. For this I had to use the Tiny website (**http://tinyurl.com**) to shorten the web address to **http://tinyurl.com/yjwzbd6** – without doing so, it would be some 578 characters long!

A huge thank you to Simon Fowler for suggesting that I have a go at this book and for his many comments subsequently on the text; to Rupert Harding for eternal patience in awaiting its delivery; to Brian Elliott for his skilful editing of the material; to the many genealogists, students, blog readers and more who have been in touch to alert me to new developments online; and most importantly to my wife Claire, and sons Calum and Jamie, for their eternal support.

On a final note, the internet can be a volatile beast, as websites come and websites go. All links in this book were correct at the time of writing (autumn 2010), but if a link is found to be broken, try searching for the same collection with a search engine, as it may well be that the site has migrated to a new web domain. Occasionally sites will temporarily go down only to reappear later down the line, and in some cases you may well be able to retrieve an earlier version of a site that has expired on sites such as the Wayback Machine.

Chapter One

GATEWAYS AND INSTITUTIONS

Genealogical information comes in the form of both primary and secondary sources, and the wealth of information found online is no different. Primary sources are original documents and recordings, whilst secondary sources are those which provide a story 'second hand' or which create a 'finding aid' to the original. It is always preferable to find a primary source, to see for yourself the most immediate record of any event.

It is worth bearing in mind that all documentary records can only be as good as the information given to the writer who presented his or her account of the proceedings. Records can in fact mislead – a wrong age given by the vain, an incorrect marital status by the serial bigamist, a false claim to the aristocracy in the name of social advancement. It is therefore important to check and double check any records found wherever possible against other sources.

Also bear in mind that you may find an entry for someone in an index with the right name in the right location at the right time, but that that does not necessarily mean you have found the right person. In times past, the pool of personal names was more limited, and you may not be looking at a complete record set.

Sometimes when we experience problems, the fault is not with the record or the website, but in our expectations. Surnames have not always been spelt the same way, for example, and geographical boundaries have changed constantly across time. We may need to be more lateral in our approach, by using name variants, wildcards and other search techniques, or by being better educated about the environments within which our ancestors lived.

Understanding the nature of the records found on a website, and the scope of the material included, is extremely important. Above all, despite its great strengths and advantages, never forget that not everything *is* online, and what is not yet available on the internet can be equally as important as what is.

Recording information

No matter which websites you consult, keep a note of their addresses and what information you have gleaned from them. You can save website addresses ('URLs') on your browser's *Favourites* tool, saving you having to retype the addresses on future visits. Be aware that some may change from time to time, particularly with those from local authorities, and that information remains online in most cases only so long as the host platform is still around, or whilst the person who created the resource is still maintaining it.

It is always advisable to make a copy of any information discovered as soon as you find it. You can type out relevant portions, cut and paste text, save the web page as a file to be consulted offline, print off the page, or take 'screen grabs' (using your 'Print Screen' button). If a site does go down for any reason, all may still not be lost – some sites such as the Internet Archive's *Wayback Machine* (**www.archive.org**) actually save many sites for posterity at regular intervals, allowing you to see earlier versions of the page before its eventual demise.

You can choose to save your family tree and your research notes online through various genealogical social networking sites or online tree providers (see p. 184). Be wary of what you place online however, most notably when it comes to the issue of privacy. Some people may not be happy about having their family details made available for all to see; some vendors will in fact not allow it and prevent such information from being made public. Others will offer a facility to share your family history project only with those that you have invited to participate. As a rough rule of thumb, do not place details of people online who are still alive and/or born less than a century ago and you should be covered.

Gateway sites

There are many free 'gateway sites' that can help you to locate useful resources for your research. For the lay of the land with regard to the location of the archives, libraries and records in the British and Irish genealogical world, the multilayered GENUKI website (**www.genuki. com**) is the grandfather of them all. This allows you to search at several regional levels for resources, and includes details for the Channel Islands and the Isle of Man, as well as the UK and the Republic of Ireland. It also includes the GENEVA genealogical event listings page, mailing lists, and many other projects. Its strength depends on the input of the local co-ordinators, with some regions providing fairly basic information, and others providing the most extraordinary details. Similar to GENUKI are British Isles GenWeb (**www.britishislesgenweb.org**) and the UK and Ireland Genealogy Search pages (**www.ukisearch.com**).

The 'UK' family of sites from Ian and Sharon Hartas are a series of free to access directories providing links to resources from both a county or subject based search. They include UK Births, Marriages and Deaths (**www.ukbmd.org.uk**), UK Genealogical Directories and Lists (**www. ukgdl.org.uk**), and UK Military Family History (**www.ukmfh.org.uk**).

UKBMD is a constantly updated directory site for British resources. Courtesy of the UKBMD Project

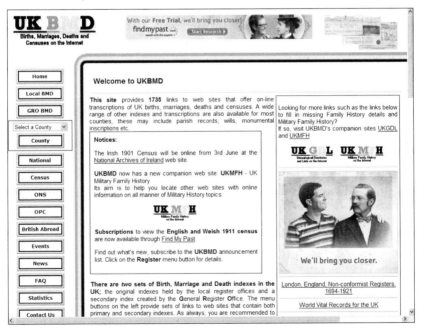

There is a degree of overlap to the links reported between the sites, but all should be consulted. Other worthwhile sites are Cyndi's List (**www.cyndislist.com**), a vast directory of resources which provides links to all the latest genealogical websites, blogs and forums, which is searchable both geographically and thematically, and Relative Links (**www.riggs.org.uk/Links/Wales.htm**).

Specifically for England, a useful list of over 500 useful sites is hosted at the Price and Associates website (**http://pricegen.com/english_genealogy. html**), whilst the Scotland's Family site (**www. scotlandsfamily.com**) is also worth visiting for resources such as parish maps and records indexes.

Ireland is well served by the Fianna web project (**www.rootsweb. ancestry.com/~fianna/county/index1.html**), the Irish Ancestors site (**www.irishtimes.com/ancestor/browse/counties**), the From Ireland pages (**www.from-ireland.net**) and the Irish Genealogical Project (**www.igp-web.com**). On a pay per view basis Irish Family History (**www.irishfamilyresearch.co.uk**) has many impressive databases.

The Mormon Church has gone to extraordinary lengths to secure and photograph copies of records from around the world, including parish records, probate papers, maps and more. Its FamilySearch website (**www.familysearch.org**) importantly hosts the *International Genealogical Index* (see p. 20), but also a powerful catalogue of its resources which can be ordered and consulted on microfilm. The site also has a useful 'wiki' based section with articles on various subjects, and a new *Record Search Pilot* site where materials are being digitised and placed online for free.

Key Institutions
There are many important national repositories across the United Kingdom which hold a great deal of genealogical material, and which are increasingly finding ways to make their holdings accessible online.

National archives
The National Archives (TNA) is the main archive repository for the United Kingdom, predominantly for material from England and Wales, though covering all four nations. Its website at **www.nationalarchives. gov.uk** contains various research and resource guides, digitised records via its Documents Online service (see p. 12), downloadable lecture podcasts and its main holdings catalogue. Several other important catalogues are also hosted on the site, such as the Manorial Documents

The National Archives website. Courtesy of The National Archives

Register (**http://nationalarchives.gov.uk/mdr**) and the Hospital Records Database (**http://nationalarchives.gov.uk/hospitalrecords**). For several years the institution has been forming strategic partnerships with many online commercial vendors in order to digitise its most commonly used materials – a full list is available at **www.nationalarchives.gov.uk/records/catalogues-and-online-records.htm**.

The National Archives of Scotland (NAS) is the equivalent repository north of the border. It does not host digitised records on its site at **www.nas.gov.uk**, but does carry an impressive catalogue and many detailed guides. The facility is digitising some resources in partnership with other bodies and making them available through sites such as ScotlandsPeople (see below), ScotlandsPlaces (p. 33) and Scottish Documents (**www.scottishdocuments.com**), most notably wills, maps and church records.

The Public Record Office of Northern Ireland (PRONI) is freely providing a wealth of digitised genealogical materials on its site at **www.proni.gov.uk**, including the 1912 Ulster Covenant, street directories, a wills database and Name Search facility, freeholders' records, and an online catalogue, as well as several downloadable resources guides.

The National Archives of Ireland (**www.nationalarchives.ie**) has many databases on its site, including an *Ireland to Australia Transportation Database*, a *Directory of Sources for Women's History in Ireland* and *Famine Relief Commission Papers*, as well as several research guides. In partnership with Library and Archives Canada (p. 178) the institution has also digitised the surviving census returns for 1901 and 1911 and placed them online (see p. 25).

Local archives
The ultimate locator for locally based archives in the UK is the ARCHON Directory (**www.nationalarchives.gov.uk/archon**), which provides links to websites, contact details, and some information on holdings. Equally useful is the Ancestor Search site (**www.ancestor-search.info/ LOC-INDEX.htm**) which provides directory information for all county-based libraries, record offices, family history societies and research centres.

Many locally based archives, museums and libraries in England and Wales are making their catalogues accessible via a central search facility entitled Access to Archives or 'A2A' (**www.nationalarchives. gov.uk/a2a**), with the Scottish Archives Network (**www.scan.org.uk**) the northern equivalent. The National Register of Archives (**www. nationalarchives.gov.uk/nra**) is a database listing some 44,000 unpublished lists and catalogues detailing the locations of additional material held across the UK, much of it in private hands, and again, there is a Scottish equivalent, the National Register of Archives of Scotland (**www.nas.gov.uk/onlineregister**). In Ireland you can use the Research and Special Collections Available Locally database, or 'RASCAL' (**www.rascal.ac.uk**).

Further centralised searches can be performed at the Archives Hub (**www.archiveshub.ac.uk**), representing collections from 180 academic institutions across the UK, and the Gateway to Archives of Scottish Higher Education site (**www.gashe.ac.uk**). The Archives Wales (Archifau Cymru) site (**www.archivesnetworkwales.info**) allows a keyword search through records held in 21 archives across the country, and Community Archives Wales (**www.ourwales.org.uk**) holds many locally digitised collections. For Greater London, the Archives in London and the M25 Area (AIM25) facility at **www.aim25.ac.uk** provides a useful gateway.

Libraries
The British Library in London holds over 14 million books, and millions of journals, patents, sound recordings and more. Its website (**www.bl.uk**) hosts several online exhibitions, catalogues and digitised examples from its holdings, whilst there are also several dedicated sites for particular collections such as its newspaper holdings or its Indian records holdings, some of which require a subscription. A useful page to bookmark is the *Help for Researchers* section at **www.bl.uk/reshelp/ findhelprestype/catblhold/all/allcat.html**, which lists all of the facility's online catalogues.

The National Library of Scotland (**www.nls.uk**) hosts many equally important collections, including one of the best mapping collections online in the UK, and other fascinating sections, for example the *Scottish History in Print* area at **www.nls.uk/print/index.html** with various transcribed historic publications.

The National Library of Wales (**www.llgc.org.uk**) has an equally well developed online presence with many useful catalogues and digitised collections, including wills, the National Screen and Sound Archives of Wales (at **www.archif.com**) and more. The site is very family history friendly, and probably the easiest to navigate around.

Amongst the offerings of The National Library of Ireland (**www.nli.ie**) there is the Sources database (**http://sources.nli.ie**), which lists names found in manuscripts held by the institution up to 1980 and in over 150 periodical titles up to 1969, and its Digital Photographs Online collection (**http://digital.nli.ie/cdm4/index_glassplates.php?CISOROOT=/ glassplates**).

Societies
The umbrella bodies for family history societies in the UK are the Federation of Family History Societies (**www.ffhs.org.uk**), the Scottish Association of Family History Societies (**www.safhs.org.uk**), the Association of Family History Societies of Wales (**www.fhswales.org. uk**) and the North of Ireland Family History Society (**www.nifhs.org**). Not every society in the country will be affiliated to these however. In the Western Isles of Scotland, for example, societies known in Gaelic as *comainn eachdraidh* exist independently – a general list of these can be found at **www.smo.uhi.ac.uk/gaidhlig/buidhnean/eachdraidh**. Most society sites have some online resources, though they vary considerably in what they provide.

Several genealogical societies exist also with developed online platforms. The London based Society of Genealogists (**www.sog.org.uk**) hosts a catalogue of its library holdings, and various databases for members only; the Edinburgh based Scottish Genealogy Society (**www.scotsgenealogy.com**) has an online *Family History Index* outlining some of the private papers which have been deposited with the body, as well as a discussion forum (**www.yabbers.com/phpbb/scotsgen.html**); and the Ulster Historical Foundation (**www.ancestryireland.com**) has many databases online exclusively for members.

Local History Online (**www.local-history.co.uk**) also provides details of history societies across the British Isles, many of which have useful web resources, whilst the British Association for Local History site may also help (**www.balh.co.uk**).

Commercial vendors

Family history is a fairly competitive business for vendors, offering a vast range of genealogically useful online materials either by subscription or on a pay-per-view basis. The following are the largest and will be constantly referred to throughout the book.

Ancestry www.ancestry.co.uk

Ancestry.co.uk is the UK arm of the American based Ancestry.com corporation, and it is probably fair to say that you would be almost guaranteed to find something on the site of use to your family history, no matter where in the British Isles you might be from. Amongst its most useful and impressive holdings are:

- Birth, Marriage and Death Indexes (England and Wales)
- National Probate Calendar (England and Wales)
- UK Census Collection (excluding Ireland)
- British Army WW1 Service records
- UK Parish Records Collections
- London Historical Records Collection
- Immigration and Emigration records

The site also hosts online discussion forums and users' family trees.

FindmyPast www.findmypast.co.uk

FindmyPast.co.uk is owned by Brightsolid Ltd, and focuses primarily on English and Welsh records, though some collections are useful for the entire United Kingdom. Its major holdings include:

Ancestry.co.uk is the largest online commercial genealogy vendor in the UK.
Courtesy of Ancestry.co.uk

- Births, Marriages and Deaths 1538–2006 (England and Wales)
- England and Wales Censuses 1841–1911
- UK Migration Records 1793–1960
- British Army Service Records 1760–1913

The site exclusively provides access to the 1911 English and Welsh census, which can also be viewed via its subsidiary site at **www. 1911census.com**. Whilst competing against Ancestry in providing some of the same mainstream vital records and censuses collections, it also has a great deal of content unique to its site such as its Great Western Shareholders 1835–1932, and also provides a family tree hosting facility.

The Genealogist **www.thegenealogist.co.uk**
The Genealogist is another site primarily useful for English and Welsh research, with a handful of Scottish and Irish resources. The site has a loyal volunteer transcriber community helping to index its census and

parish records collections, and runs many digitisation projects with partners, such as PCC wills and nonconformist records collections from TNA. Its major collections include:

- Birth, Marriage and Death Indexes (England and Wales)
- Parish records
- Non-Conformist and Non-Parochial records
- Directories

A subsidiary site, **www.bmdregisters.com**, also carries its unique non-conformist records collections. The site can host user submitted family trees via its free to use Tree Builder software.

Documents Online **www.nationalarchives.gov.uk/documentsonline**
Documents Online provides digitised records from TNA at Kew on a pay-per-view basis from the institution's holdings in downloadable PDF files, most notably for naval records and PCC wills (see p. 27).

Origins Network **www.origins.net**
The Origins Network provides various resources for British and Irish research, available in separate subscription packages – *Total Access* for all of its holdings; *Irish Origins* for records in Ireland; *British Origins* for English and Welsh resources; and the free to access *Scots Origins*. The latter hosts no records as such, but offers some excellent online tools to help with Scottish research.

WorldVitalRecords **www.worldvitalrecords.com**
The American based WorldVitalRecords is increasingly providing British and Irish content on its site through its World Collection sub-scription, and has many interesting collections, most notably parish records material and its *Paper of Record* newspaper series, with some UK titles.

FamilyRelatives **www.familyrelatives.com**
FamilyRelatives.com offers records for the UK, Ireland, and elsewhere in the world by subscription, as well as social networking tools and an online family tree hosting capability. Amongst its collections military research materials, parish records, and free access to the GRO's overseas birth, marriage and death indexes (p. 18).

Genes Reunited **www.genesreunited.com**
Genes Reunited hosts user submitted family trees and offers a powerful networking tool for those seeking to find connections with relatives. It works by allowing you to upload your family tree, or to create a tree from scratch, and to then alert you to potential 'hot' matches between the data in your family tree and that found on others, though the definition of 'hot' can sometimes be open to question! The site also offers some records resources, primarily for English and Welsh research, such as censuses and BMD indexes.

The Original Record **www.theoriginalrecord.com**
The Original Record has millions of useful records on its site, though has a somewhat unusual access set up. The site allows you to perform searches by surname and year – you can buy an annual subscription for searches based on that surname for £100, or for two surnames for £180, and so on, though you can also purchase individual records. It can be pricey, but a great deal of rare material hosted on the site is not available elsewhere.

ScotlandsPeople **www.scotlandspeople.gov.uk**
The ScotlandsPeople website is a joint venture between the General Register Office for Scotland, the NAS, the Court of the Lord Lyon and Brightsolid. Uniquely in the UK, it offers digitised images of the civil registration records for births, marriages and deaths, and is the only site to offer digitised images for the Scottish censuses. Other holdings include Church of Scotland and Roman Catholic parish records, wills and records on Scottish heraldry.

Chapter Two

GENEALOGICAL ESSENTIALS

Before adding the flesh to your family tree, it helps to establish the bones, and in this chapter I will look at the core basic records and sites that will help you to get your research well underway.

Births, marriages and deaths

England and Wales
Civil registration of English and Welsh births, marriages and deaths commenced on July 1 1837, and copies of certificates can be obtained from two main sources – the General Register Office of England and Wales (**www.direct.gov.uk/gro**), and local superintendent registrars' offices. Whenever a record was registered locally, it was indexed by that registration office, but copies were also sent to the national GRO every three months up to 1983, and annually from 1984, from which the national GRO then compiled its own indexes. The two sets of indexes are not compatible, and so a local index entry cannot be used to order from the national GRO, and vice versa. Barbara Dixon's detailed overview on the different types of certificate and the information you will find in them can be read at **http://home.clara.net/dixons/Certificates/indexbd.htm**.

The easiest way to search for civil registration events is to use the national GRO indexes. The volunteer based FreeBMD website (**www.freebmd.org.uk**) is working to provide free transcriptions and images of the indexes from 1837 to 1983. At the time of writing the database is almost complete up to 1931, though coverage tails off markedly after that.

Records for births, marriages and deaths have been recorded by the state since 1837, and are available through many sites. Author's collection

FreeBMD's indexes up to 1915 can also be accessed at Ancestry, which has created its own indexes thereafter to 2005. Of all the commercial vendors, Ancestry and FindmyPast have the most developed search facilities, allowing searches of transcriptions of the individual index

Family Relatives is just one of many commercial sites offering access to the national GRO BMD indexes. Courtesy of FamilyRelatives.com

records by name, year, quarter, mother's maiden name, and registration district. As with any transcriptions though, the indexes are not immune to errors. The GRO index pages are also available at FamilyRelatives, the Genealogist and GenesReunited, but are more cumbersome to search through.

Once you find the right entry, take a note of the reference number and then order the record from the GRO at **www.gro.gov.uk/gro/content/certificates**, for a standard rate of £9.25 per record. Always order certificates directly from the GRO, as some online vendors can charge up to three times the cost per certificate if ordered through them.

As noted, the national indexes were compiled from copies of the original local registers. Errors sometimes occurred in this process, and so you may find that the local registrar has the record even if you cannot find it nationally. Records are also slightly cheaper to obtain locally, at £9 each. Not every local registration office has placed its index online, but many are increasingly doing so. To find out if this is the case, consult UKBMD (**www.ukbmd.org.uk**) or your local council website.

Several certificate exchange sites exist where people are willing to swap details of certificates already purchased. These include **www. certificate-exchange.co.uk**, **http://bmd-cert-exch-site.ourwardfamily.com**, **http://aztecrose.tripod.com/LookupExchange.htm**, and in Scotland, **www.sctbdm.com**. All are worth checking, as you may well share a family connection with the person who uploaded a record that you are interested in.

Scotland

Scottish civil registration commenced in 1855, and is administered by the General Register Office for Scotland (GROS) at **www.gro-scotland. gov.uk**. For a background to its establishment, consult *The Scottish Way of Birth and Death* (**www.gla.ac.uk/departments/scottishwayofbirthand death**).

The records of civil births, marriages and deaths have been digitised and made partially available online at the ScotlandsPeople website. Whilst this contains indexes up to the modern period, it operates an online closure policy for many of the actual records, meaning that full birth record entries for the last 100 years cannot be viewed, nor marriages for the last 75 years or deaths for the last 50. The indexes for these most recent records are also more restrictive in the detail carried, but can be used to order up official printed extracts from the GROS.

The records include many minor collections such as overseas military death registrations and the *Register for Corrected Entries*, though this cannot be searched as a database in its own right (a link to the register is highlighted if mentioned in a civil record). Civil birth and marriage records from 1855–1875 are also indexed on FamilySearch's *International Genealogical Index* database. Whilst Scottish divorce records cannot be consulted online, a useful research guide on divorce is available from the NAS (**www.nas.gov.uk/guides/divorce.asp**).

If your Scottish ancestor moved to England, consult the Manchester and Lancashire Family History Society website (**www.mlfhs.org.uk**) which has placed a helpful database online for marriages where at least one of the spouses was Scottish, and noting from where in Scotland he or she originated.

Ireland

Civil registration commenced in Ireland in 1845, but only for non-Catholic marriages. It was not until January 1864 that a full system was introduced for all births, marriages and deaths, similar to that in Britain, with copies of all locally registered events going to the national GRO at Dublin. Following Partition in 1922, the GRO in Dublin continued to record information for the south, whilst the GRO in Belfast did likewise for the north.

The majority of civil records indexes for the whole island from 1845 to 1922 are transcribed and freely available at FamilySearch's *Record Pilot Search* site (**http://pilot.familysearch.org**) – for the Republic, additional indexes up to 1958 are also available. The information from these can be used to order up photocopied extracts from the current southern GRO (**www.groireland.ie**). This includes all records for the north up to 1922.

For events in the north after Partition, you can apply online for records through the Northern Irish GRO website (**www.groni.gov.uk**). Events before 1922 can be ordered here also, but are more expensive to obtain than from the south. A digitisation project is currently underway for all registered events, which will also see the creation of new indexes. Births from 1864–1874, and some early marriages, are indexed on the *International Genealogical Index* (see p. 20).

British subjects overseas

If your ancestor moved abroad, check FamilyRelatives for freely hosted indexes of consular and overseas records, as well as Chaplains' returns for overseas regiments, with events recorded as recently as 2005. These too can be ordered from the GRO (**www.gro.gov.uk/gro/content/ certificates**), though via a separate online application form. Many of the indexes are also hosted at FindmyPast and the Genealogist websites, with the latter also having additional records from the *General Register Office: Miscellaneous Foreign Returns* (1831–1964) collection at TNA (RG 32). This includes vital records as recorded on British, as well as foreign, ships, and of British subjects and British colonial and Commonwealth nationals from around the world. Not all overseas events are online – some are held within consular registers at TNA – but the online collections do represent a significant proportion of what exists.

Adoption and children

For advice concerning adoption issues, visit Adoption Search Reunion (**www.adoptionsearchreunion.org.uk**), or in Scotland, Birthlink (**www. birthlink.org.uk**). You can also register an interest with the UK Birth

Adoption Register (**www.ukbirth-adoptionregister.com**), after paying a £10 registration fee. At the time of writing, the site had just initiated its 1332nd reunion in its eighth year.

For British children keen to trace their Canadian birth fathers from the Second World War, visit Canadian Roots UK (**www.canadianrootsuk. org**), whilst the Child Migrants Trust (**www.childmigrantstrust.com**) tries to help reunite children sent by the British Government to Canada, New Zealand, Australia and Rhodesia from the end of the Second World War to the early 1970s with their birth families.

If your ancestor spent time at the Foundling Hospital in London visit **www.foundlingmuseum.org.uk/oralhistory.php**. A genealogy service is available through **www.quarriers.org.uk** to trace records of Scottish street children who stayed in Quarriers Homes, whilst homeless and destitute boys who were sent to the Mars Training Ship in Dundee can be researched at **www.sonsofthemars.com**. Missing Ancestors (**http:// missing-ancestors.com**) also provides resources to help trace children who may have gone missing from your tree.

Surnames

There are several surname websites seeking to provide explanations as to the origins of individual names, but many of them need to be taken with a pinch of salt! If I do a search on my own surname of Paton, the British Surnames site (**www.britishsurnames.co.uk**) tells me that the name is Spanish; the Internet Surname Database (**www.surnamedb. com**) informs me that it comes from one of two possible origins, one being English, the other French. I assume my Scottish ancestors would be turning in their graves!

The Guild of One-Name Studies, known affectionately to many as the 'GOONS', is a body of dedicated volunteers who have each undertaken to study a single surname in records from across the English speaking world. A list of over 2000 names being studied by the organisation is available at **www.one-name.org/register.html**.

Church records

In the pre-civil registration period, we need to rely on parochial records for evidence of our ancestors' lives. The state church in England, Wales and Ireland was the Anglican Church, whilst in Scotland it was the Presbyterian based Church of Scotland.

Bear in mind that our ancestors often moved from parish to parish, and could be considerably more mobile then we give them credit for. To understand which parishes may adjoin the 'home' parish, use the Parish Finder website (**www.parishfinder.co.uk**). There are many sites depicting places of worship across the British Isles, such as the Churches of Britain and Ireland website at **www.churches-uk-ireland.org**.

Parish registers

There is no one single source holding all parish records online. The most comprehensive is perhaps the *International Genealogical Index* (IGI) at FamilySearch (**www.familysearch.org**). This provides a free index to Church of England baptisms and marriages up to 1837, and often beyond, as well as many returns for non-conformist churches, with Scottish records also included up to 1854. The index has been created from registers microfilmed by the Church of Jesus Christ of Latter Day Saints, with each film given a batch number, and using these numbers, searches can also be performed in the IGI via Hugh Wallis's site at **http://freepages.genealogy.rootsweb.ancestry.com/~hughwallis/**

The International Genealogy Index. Courtesy of of FamilySearch.org copyright by Intellectual Reserve, Inc by permission

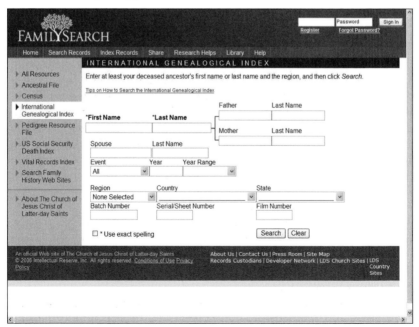

IGIBatchNumbers.htm. Scottish parish level searches can also be carried out through the Origins Network site at **www.origins.net/ScotsOrigins/SOUserHome.aspx**. Once an index entry is found the original record should always be consulted.

FamilySearch is also making material freely available through its Records Search Pilot website (**http://pilot.familysearch.org**). This includes its *England Baptisms* and *England Marriages* databases from 1700–1900, and various digitised regional records, as part of a long term project to make records held centrally on microfilm by the Mormons at the Granite Mountain Vault in Utah available online.

All of the Church of Scotland's surviving parish registers, dating as far back as 1553, have been digitised and made available through the ScotlandsPeople website. Digitised kirk session material, the equivalent of English vestry records, will also be made available in due course, with the upload of Roman Catholic records already underway. At the time of writing Catholic baptisms were already online, with many other collections due to follow throughout 2011. Of particular note is the *Bishopric of the Forces* collection which not only covers Scotland, but also provides Catholic records for military bases in England and overseas.

The Church of Scotland was prone to splits and reunions, seemingly thriving on theological disruption routinely from the Reformation. Few records of the dissenting faiths are online as yet, though in some cases you will find dissenting church records in Church of Scotland registers (if the minister felt inclined). A summary of the main splits is available at **www.scotlandsgreateststory.bravehost.com/scottishkirk.html**. Another fascinating database for Scottish research concerns a group heavily persecuted by the Kirk from the sixteenth to eighteenth centuries. The Survey of Scottish Witchcraft (**www.shc.ed.ac.uk/Research/witches**) has details of nearly 4000 people tried from 1563–1736 for witchcraft, with evidence for many gathered by local kirk sessions.

FreeREG (**www.freereg.org.uk**) also allows for searches of many church baptisms, marriages and burials from across Britain. It provides more details than the IGI, but is not as complete. In Wales, marriage allegations and bonds have been indexed from 1661–1837 by the National Library of Wales and can be searched via its online catalogue (**http://isys.llgc.org.uk**).

The commercial websites offer a great deal of parish register material. FindmyPast's *Parish Records Collection 1538–2005*, produced in association with the Federation of Family History Societies, includes most of the second edition of the *National Burial Index*, providing an index to information compiled from various registers by family history societies across England and Wales. The Genealogist also offers English and Welsh holdings; of particular note is its non-conformist records collection, including events recorded by Presbyterians, Congregationalists, Baptists, Quakers, Methodists, Unitarians and the Russian Orthodox Church, as well as records of clandestine marriages and baptisms performed at the Fleet prison from 1667–1777. The same collection is accessible at **www.bmdregisters.co.uk**.

Ancestry's *UK Parish Baptism, Marriage and Burial Records* collection contains British records extracted from the 1500s to the 1900s, including many Scottish returns (Episcopalian, Catholic etc). Ancestry also has many standalone databases for parish records across the country, such as *Breconshire, Welsh marriages 1813–1837*, and its new *London Parish Records Collection*, produced in association with the London Metropolitan Archives, which when completely released will contain records from over a thousand Greater London parishes. The Origins Network hosts *Boyd's Marriage Index* for England from 1538 to 1840, featuring some 7 million entries from across the country, mainly in London and Middlesex, estimated to be 15% of all events in that period. The site also has records for London and Dorset.

The Public Records Office of Northern Ireland has made available a guide on its church records holdings at **www.proni.gov.uk/ guide_to_church_records.pdf**. The National Library of Ireland has a similar guide at **www.nli.ie/en/parish-register.aspx**, whilst at **www. irishtimes.com/ancestor/browse/counties/rcmaps** the *Irish Times* hosts an interactive map leading to individual Catholic parishes and the availability of records within each. The main online source for accessing transcriptions of parish material in Ireland, north and south, is the Irish Family History Foundation site (**www.rootsireland.ie**). This carries transcribed Roman Catholic, Church of Ireland and Presbyterian parish records, and some county based civil records, with transcriptions costing €5 each to access at the time of writing. The equally useful subscription based Emerald Ancestors (**www.emeraldancestors.com**) has index databases for Northern Irish births (1796–1924), marriages (1823–1922) and deaths (1803–1900), from both church and civil registration records. The indexed information returned is quite generous, with an ordering service available for fully transcribed extracts.

Gravestones and burials

Several sites provide access to transcriptions and/or photographs of gravestone inscriptions, including Interment.net (**www.interment.net**), Gravestone Photos (**www.gravestonephotos.com**) and the Wishful Thinking GENUKI section (**www.wishful-thinking.org.uk/genuki**). To understand gravestones written in Welsh, John Ball's site (**www.jlb2005. plus.com/wales/welsh-phrases.htm**) provides a handy translation for some of the most common words found.

The Scottish Graveyards Project (**www.scottishgraveyards.org.uk**) is recording and conserving many grave sites across the country, whilst Find a Grave in Scotland (**www.findagraveinscotland.com**), Scottish Monumental Inscriptions (**www.scottish-monumental-inscriptions. com**) and Memento Mori (**www.memento-mori.co.uk**) carry many other northern records. The History from Headstones project (**www. historyfromheadstones.com**) has about 50,000 inscriptions from over 800 graveyards in Northern Ireland, whilst the North of Ireland Family History Society operates a members' look-up scheme for graveyards which it is recording (**www.nifhs.org/lookups.htm**).

Deceased Online (**www.deceasedonline.com**) is slowly digitising burial records from across the British Isles and making them available on a pay-per-view basis. At the time of writing, the site had uploaded records from several London boroughs, Aberdeen, the whole of Angus in Scotland, and crematorium records for Kent and Sussex.

Other resources

The JewishGen site (**www.jewishgen.org/databases/UK**) contains over 60,000 records for Jewish marriages and burials, as well as census details. A handful of marriage contracts written in Aramaic can also be found at **http://jnul.huji.ac.il/dl/ketubbot/html/UnitedKingdom.htm**, whilst the United Synagogue site (**www.theus.org.uk**) has two useful databases, the first containing over 8000 Jewish marriages from 1880–1891, the other containing burial records from twelve southern English based cemeteries. For Jewish research in Ireland visit **www.jewishireland. org/genealogy.html**, and for Scotland visit **www.sjac.org.uk**.

The Quaker Family History Society (**www.qfhs.co.uk**) provides links to Meetings records from across Britain, whilst the Library of the Religious Society of Friends has an online catalogue for its holdings (**www. quaker.org.uk/search-catalogue**). The Genealogist website has made available records concerning Quakers in its nonconformist collection, whilst the Yorkshire Quaker Heritage Project has also compiled a list of useful sources from across Britain (**www.hull.ac.uk/oldlib/archives/ quaker/archon.htm**). For Ireland, visit **www.quakers-in-ireland.org**.

A gateway site for many archives and repositories relating to the Roman Catholic Church can be found at **www.catholic-history. org.uk**, and the catalogue for the Catholic National Library at **www. catholic-library.org.uk**. The Catholic Encyclopaedia may also assist at **www.newadvent.org/cathen/01729a.htm**.

Censuses

A decennial census has been recorded in Britain from 1801, though the 1841 census was the first to be genealogically useful in listing names of those present in each household.

Most of the main genealogical vendors offer access to digitised copies of the original returns from 1841–1901 for England and Wales. The Genealogist, as is common with many service providers, outsourced its indexing overseas, but soon after introduced a popular volunteer transcription project at **www.ukindexer.co.uk**, allowing users to gain free credits for use on its website by correcting some of the many errors found in the transcribed returns. Ancestry has transcription errors on its site for similar reasons, but invites users to submit corrections through a facility on its site. On GenesReunited, a useful feature is the ability to consult a map for the census location returned on a particular search. The Origins Network also hosts the 1841, 1861 and 1871 returns.

In 2009, FindmyPast exclusively published the 1911 census returns for England and Wales via a pay-per-view website at **www.1911census. co.uk**, and later through its main website. The census differs from its predecessors in that the original multi-page household schedules have survived, written in most cases by our ancestors themselves, and not just the enumerators' returns normally encountered. FindmyPast is also the only vendor to provide access to the 1851 Manchester area census.

Scottish census returns from 1841–1901 have been digitised and the images made exclusively available at ScotlandsPeople. The site also carries a transcript of the 1881 census (created by the Mormons) which is cheaper to view than the digitised equivalent. The only other source for the complete Scottish census is Ancestry, though in transcription form only. Not all information is returned however – questions such as ability to speak Gaelic and/or English (from 1891), and marital status, are not included. The 1911 census for Scotland will not be available until April 2011 at the earliest, and unlike its British and Irish counterparts,

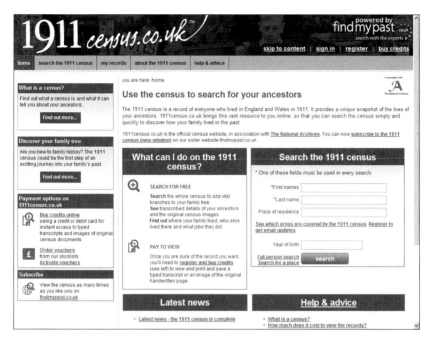

Access to the English and Welsh 1911 Census. Courtesy of FindmyPast.co.uk

the information is to be made accessible via the two page long enumerators' returns and not the household schedules.

FreeCEN (**www.freecen.org.uk**) is a volunteer run project painstakingly transcribing the records from 1841 to 1891. Its English returns are more complete for the latter censuses from 1861 onwards, there is little available for Wales, and Scottish coverage tends to favour 1841 and 1851. FamilySearch also hosts an index to the 1881 census returns for England and Wales, whilst the Workhouse website (**www.workhouses.org**) also carries free transcriptions for each workhouse and poorhouse in the same census.

Census Finder (**www.censusfinder.com**) provides details of many locally hosted transcription projects, including some pre-1841 returns which contain genealogically useful material. The site also provides links to returns for directories, freeholder records, militia lists and other census substitutes for the pre-1801 period.

Although part of the UK, the Irish census in fact first commenced in 1821, and with genealogically useful information from the outset. Unfortunately, due to a combination of deliberate pulping by the British

Government and later destruction during the Irish Civil War, only the 1901 and 1911 returns have largely survived. These have been digitised and made freely available by the National Archives of Ireland at **www.census.nationalarchives.ie**. If your Irish ancestor was in Britain when the censuses were recorded, check the North of Ireland Family History Society's strays site (**www.nifhs.org/straysA.htm**).

Copies of some Irish entries have survived from 1841 and 1851, used to provide evidence for people wishing to claim a state pension in 1909. The northern returns can be accessed at **www.pensear.org** or at **www.emeraldancestors.com**. Ancestry hosts the equivalent for the Republic, as well as the 1851 Antrim census, a great deal of which has survived, and the 1766 Religious Census of Ireland. Some other surviving returns, mainly from 1821, can be located through Census Finder (see earlier). Although most censuses have been lost, several substitutes do exist. The most useful is Griffith's Valuation, a land valuation taken in the mid nineteenth century across the island, which is freely available at **www.askaboutireland.ie/griffith-valuation**. Also online is a census for the island from 1659 at **http://clanmaclochlainn. com/1659cen.htm**. The PRONI website also includes surviving fragments of the 1740 and the 1766 religious census returns in its *Names Search* database.

Statistical information from the censuses can be extremely enlightening. A Vision of Britain Through Time (**www.visionofbritain.org.uk**) hosts reports for the censuses from 1801–1971, with a similar site entitled Histpop available at **www.histpop.org**. For the Republic of Ireland, the equivalent reports from 1926–1999 are available at **www. cso.ie/census/historical_reports.htm**. The Genealogist site also hosts a Surname Concentration Maps facility which plots the frequency of surnames in each English and Welsh county as noted in the censuses from 1841–1901. For 1881 and 1998, the National Trust provides a similar tool at **www.nationaltrustnames.org.uk**. For Ireland, data derived from Robert Matheson's *Special Report on Surnames* in 1890 can be used to plot a surname distribution at **www.ancestryireland.com/ database.php?filename=db_mathesons**.

Probate and Confirmation
Wills and inventories can usefully provide information on how your ancestors once lived, but can often be difficult to find. The systems for probate vary considerably across the UK, being proved or confirmed in a variety of different courts.

England and Wales

Probate for English and Welsh wills was granted by various courts of the hierarchical Church of England up to 1858, and can be a nightmare to locate. You may be lucky enough to find a copy of your record of interest at a volunteer based exchange site for wills, such as **www.willtranscriptions.co.uk**.

The two highest probate courts in the land were the Prerogative Court of Canterbury (PCC), for the south of England and Wales, and the Prerogative Court of York (PCY) for northern England. A useful guide to the hierarchy below these courts is available at **www.nationalarchives.gov.uk/familyhistory/wills/?WT.lp=-33504**. Documents Online has the complete collection of PCC wills from 1384–1858, with records searchable by first and last names, place, occupation and date of probate. A digital copy of an original can then be downloaded in PDF format for £3.50. The Genealogist is currently digitising the collection also; its images are of considerably better resolution, and are available through a main subscription.

An exciting development at the time of writing is the new National Wills Index hosted on the Origins Network site, produced in collaboration with the British Record Society, the Borthwick Institute for Archives, the Genealogical Society of Utah and additional partners such as Oxfordshire Record Office. The plan is to provide a unique single access point for all surviving pre-1858 wills as held by the various partners, including the creation of new indexes and the digitisation of many surviving records. For the last 130 years the British Records Society has created the largest set of probate indexes already available, whilst FamilySearch has previously microfilmed most English probate documents, and so the potential for this is huge. The York based Borthwick Institute, which hosts indexes to many of its records on the Origins Network website, has already commenced the digitisation of many of its records, including records for wills granted probate through the Prerogative Court of York, the highest court in the north of England. Further partners are expected to join in due course.

Over 190,000 wills proven in the lower Welsh ecclesiastical courts prior to 1858 have been digitised and made available by the National Library of Wales at **http://tinyurl.com/yl3s9t9**. The records cannot be downloaded; copies must be ordered from the library.

From 1858 onwards, the Probate Service (**www.hmcourts-service.gov.uk/cms/wills.htm**) has run the show, part of the Family Division of the High Court. An index to its Calendar records from 1861–1941 is now

The National Wills Index on Origins.net. Courtesy of OMS Services Ltd

available on the Ancestry website. The Treasury's *Bona Vacantia* site (**www.bonavacantia.gov.uk**), used by so called 'heir hunters', contains a database of unclaimed estates which can be searched by name, place and date of death.

Another useful online resource for English and Welsh probate is the index to *Death Duty Registers 1796–1903*, published at FindmyPast. As well as providing information from the original National Archives register, which recorded the legacy duty paid on any monetary sums bequeathed in an estate, the database can also help you to identify where the original will or administration documents may have been granted probate. Digitised images from the registers from 1796–1811 are available at Documents Online.

Scotland
Prior to the Scottish Reformation, the church dealt with the 'confirmation' of wills (the equivalent of 'probate'), but the role was given to civil Commissary Courts from 1564 to the 1820s, and thereafter to the

Sheriff Courts. All records that have undergone confirmation from 1513–1901 are hosted at the ScotlandsPeople website, though this range will soon be extended further into the twentieth century later.

Note that only records placed through the confirmation process are available on the site. Other records exist for perhaps the same number of cases again, which were settled within the family or which never made it to the courts, which can be found in Registers of Deeds and Commissary Court papers. The catalogues of the NAS at **www.nas. gov.uk/onlinecatalogue** can help to locate such material, though the originals cannot be viewed online.

Ireland

A great many probate documents were destroyed during the Irish Civil War, but the surviving calendars and district registry copies for the post 1858 period for the north have been made available at the PRONI website in the form of a *Will Calendars* database. Prior to 1858, the site also offers a *Name Search* database with an index to many surviving wills and diocesan indexes held at the archive.

For the whole island, FamilyRelatives has an excellent collection of wills indexes from 1536–1857, whilst the Origins Network hosts an index from 1484–1858.

Directories

Street and trade directories can be useful in establishing the locations of people prior to the nineteenth-century censuses, and indeed, between each of the census years and beyond.

The *Historical Directories* website from the University of Leicester at **www.historicaldirectories.org** hosts several English and Welsh editions from 1750–1919, though mostly from 1850 onwards. The site does not hold complete sets for each county; Durham has twelve editions between 1801 and 1914, for example, and there are just 54 for the whole of Wales. *English Trade Directories of the nineteenth Century* (**http://tinyurl.com/4pyhmr**) is also worth consulting, containing a searchable database for sixteen counties, mainly from 1830.

Ancestry has its *UK and US Directories 1680–1830* database, a compilation of biographical extracts from various directories, including over 140 from England, (though virtually nothing for Wales), whilst its *UK City and County Directories 1600–1900* collection provides an impressive array of fully searchable digitised books for the whole of Britain. It also offers the *British Phone Books 1880–1984* collection, as sourced from the archives of British Telecom, containing some 1780 telephone directories.

The Genealogist carries a large collection of directories found via three separate search categories. Through *Directory Transcripts* you can search for Worcestershire holdings from 1790 and 1850, whilst the *Directories Records* section offers material for twenty counties for the mid nineteenth to early twentieth centuries. The most comprehensive section, however, is that simply titled *Directories*, in which there are several regional groups of directories. This has almost fifty London editions from 1677–1940, twenty-seven editions from 1828–1937 for the Midlands and East Anglia, and many others from across the country. For Wales, at the time of writing there was a disappointing two editions, being Pigot's 1844 Directories from North and South Wales, though the collections are continually being updated. FamilyRelatives also has various Pigot's Directories from the 1830s, a Slater's Trade Directory for Scotland from 1889, and a selection of medical registers and directories from 1853–1943.

The excellent *Street Directories* section of the PRONI website has many Ulster directories from 1819–1900, whilst additional holdings from 1805–1913 are found at **www.lennonwylie.co.uk**. Various county offerings from 1862 are available at **www.libraryireland.com/Genealogy.php**, whilst *The Ulster Towns Directory 1910* is online at **www.libraryireland. com/UlsterDirectory1910/Contents.php**. Additional Irish directories are available at **www.failteromhat.com**.

To trace people in more recent times, visit **www.192.com** and **http:// onlinesearches.info**, where information can be sourced from contemporary electoral registers and directories. Other localised directories can be located through gateway sites such as UKGDL, and many others will be listed in the county sections later in this book.

Maps and Gazetteers

The examination of the built environment where our ancestors once lived can help to contextualise our ancestors' stories. Changes in landscape can be plotted across time, allowing us to note the development of lines of communication such as canals, roads and railways, as well as the effects of land enclosure and the development of social housing.

Maps

The best gateway site for the discussion of maps from around the world is that run by retired British Library map librarian Tony Campbell at www.maphistory.info, though the site does not contain any images. The British Library also has an impressive introduction to the subject at **www.bl.uk/reshelp/findhelprestype/maps/index.html**.

Several sites provide current maps, including Multimap (**www. multimap.co.uk**), Streetmap (**www.streetmap.co.uk**), and Google Maps (**http://maps.google.co.uk**). The latter is particularly useful, in that in addition to the main map for an area, a satellite overview for the location, and in many cases ground level photographs ('street view'), can also be viewed. A historic aerial perspective for the country is obtainable from both **www.oldaerialphotos.com** and **http://aerial. rcahms.gov.uk**.

Britain was organised into a series of historic counties up to 1974 and a map showing their locations is at **www.abcounties.co.uk/counties/ map.htm**. The most detailed nineteenth and twentieth-century maps are those produced by the Ordnance Survey. The present collection can be viewed at the Get-a-Map service at **www.ordnancesurvey.co.uk/ oswebsite/getamap**, whilst historic examples are available from several sources. Old Maps (**www.old-maps.co.uk**) is a joint venture between the Ordnance Survey and Landmark, and carries the earliest County Series maps at 1:10 560 scale. A Vision of Britain Through Time (**www.visionofbritain.org.uk/maps**) carries the First Series of the OS for England and Wales from 1805–1869, maps from the Revised Series from 1902–05, and several British wide collections. In addition are various other maps series at different scales as recent as 1948, including county boundary maps, sanitary district maps showing civil parishes, and more. Two further sites with useful maps for Britain are Cassini Maps (**www.cassinimaps.co.uk**) and Alan Godfrey Maps (**www. alangodfreymaps.co.uk**).

Pre-dating the OS series are a set of English county maps from 1787 by John Cary, available at **http://homepage.ntlworld.com/tomals/ index11.html**. Mapseeker (**www.mapseeker.co.uk**) also carries older colour maps for some of the larger towns, cities and counties across the country, with the site also listing the sources from whence they were obtained, and a search tool for towns and villages. GENMAPS (**http:// freepages.genealogy.rootsweb.ancestry.com/~genmaps/index.html**) has an extensive old maps collection for Britain which is free to consult, whilst *Baedeker's Old Guide Books* (**http://contueor.com/baedeker/index. htm**) hosts many town plans on its site from 1910 for the whole island.

The National Library of Scotland's dedicated maps site at **www.nls. uk/maps/index.html** has over 20,000 digitised maps, including town plans from 1580 onwards, Timothy Pont's maps from the late sixteenth Century and OS returns from the mid nineteenth to early twentieth centuries. For a set of Ordnance Survey town plans from 1847–1895, visit **http://sites.scran.ac.uk/townplans/townplans.html**.

Tom's Big Chest of Old Welsh Maps (**http://homepage.ntlworld. com/tomals/Welsh-Maps-of-Samuel-Lewis,1833.htm**) contains Samuel Lewis's maps for the country from 1833, whilst John Ball's Welsh Family History Archive provides additional maps and gazetteer resources at **www.jlb2005.plus.com/wales/index.htm**, including a glossary on how to interpret Welsh place names, and a *Sounds of Wales* site, where you can hear the pronunciation of over 220 Welsh place names.

The Ordnance Survey of Northern Ireland at **https://maps.osni. gov.uk** carries both historic and current maps for the country, though registration is required for the site, and the modern Irish Ordnance Survey for the south is available at **www.osi.ie**. Historic Irish town-land maps are online at **www.pasthomes.com**, with additional historic maps for Ulster at **www.ulsterancestry.com/free-ulster-maps.html**. Several additional Irish maps are available at **www.failteromhat.com**, including a map of the Irish Free State and a road map of the island from 1877. Geograph Ireland (**www.geograph.ie**) is also trying to photo-graph every square kilometre of the island, with the results accessible via an interactive map. For Irish poor law union maps visit **www. movinghere.org.uk/deliveryfiles/PRO/MFQ1_925/0/1.pdf**.

Gazetteers

The Gazetteer of British Place Names (**www.gazetteer.co.uk**) contains information on the development of the administrative boundaries of England, as well as some historic boundary maps, whilst A Vision of Britain Through Time (**www.visionofbritain.org.uk**) carries descriptive entries from John Marius Wilson's *Imperial Gazetteer of England and Wales* (1870–72) and John Bartholomew's *Gazetteer of the British Isles* (1887), as well as many contemporary letters and documents from writers such as Daniel Defoe.

Several gazetteers are also hosted on British History Online (**www. british-history.ac.uk/source.aspx?pubid=445**), including Samuel Lewis's *Topographical Directory of England* from 1848, and various descriptive volumes for most counties as recorded by the *Victoria County History* series. A considerably more detailed Scottish equivalent for the latter is the *Statistical Accounts of Scotland* collections, drawn up between 1791–1799 and 1834–1845. These have been digitised and made available to view by the University of Edinburgh (**www.edina.ac. uk/stat-acc-scot**), by Google Books (**http://books.google.com**), and by Electric Scotland (**www.electricscotland.com**), with the latter also hosting Frances Groome's *Ordnance Survey Gazetteer for Scotland* (1896). An excellent contemporary gazetteer is Undiscovered Scotland (**www.undiscovered scotland.co.uk**), whilst a National Gazetteer for Wales is available at **http://homepage.ntlworld.com/geogdata/ngw/places.htm**.

A *Parliamentary Gazetteer of Ireland* from 1844–45 is available on Google Books (**http://tinyurl.com/ykrzc8h**), whilst the locations of Irish townlands can be established from databases at both **www.seanruad. com** and **www.ulsterancestry.com**. Another useful resource to help with placename pronunciation is the Placenames Database of Ireland (**www.logainm.ie**). For Scottish Gaelic places see **www.ainmean-aite.org**.

Heritage
For the built landscape, English Heritage (**www.english-heritage. org.uk**) has a wealth of online databases for aerial photos and the National Monuments Record. The Royal Commission on the Ancient and Historical Monuments of Wales (**www.rcahmw.gov.uk**) has a searchable database of its holdings entitled *Coflein*, whilst the Scottish equivalent, the Royal Commission on the Ancient and Historical Monuments of Scotland (**www.rcahmw.gov.uk**), has the equally useful *Canmore* and *Canmap* databases. Much of the RCAHMS material is incorporated into the new ScotlandsPlaces site (**www.scotlandsplaces. gov.uk**), which offers many free county based resources and guides, including boundary change details and tax records.

Newspapers
Newspapers are a fantastic resource for adding flesh to the bones of your ancestral tree. Useful starting points for providing details of current newspapers available in England and Wales are Online News-papers (**www.onlinenewspapers.com**) and Google's News Archive Search (**http://news.google.com/archivesearch**). The latter trawls current news sites for stories, including most British newspaper titles with an online presence, but is also producing digitised and searchable historic content from around the world over the next few years. Already included are some historic content from the *Daily Mirror* from 1953, the partially digitised *Liverpool Echo* (1886–1943), and editions of the *Glasgow Herald* from the 1930s-1960s, and late 1980s.

The British Library receives a copy of every newspaper published in the UK. An online guide to holdings is available at **www.bl.uk/ reshelp/findhelprestype/news**, and titles can be searched within the Integrated Catalogue at **http://catalogue.bl.uk/F/?func=file&file_name= login-bl-list**, through the *Newspaper Catalogue* link on the left of the page. The library has also digitised many titles from the 1800s in partnership with publishers Gale, and made them available as the subscription based *British Library nineteenth Century Newspaper Collection* website (**http://newspapers.bl.uk/blcs**). At the time of writing the site contained forty-nine local titles, mainly from England, but also including some Welsh titles, the *Glasgow Herald, Caledonian Mercury, Aberdeen Journal, Belfast Newsletter* and the *Freeman's Journal* (from Dublin). An additional twenty-two titles are also available to subscribing institutions only, which in due course will also make their way to the public site.

The library has also created the digitised *Burney Collection*, which includes early newspapers from the seventeenth – eighteenth centuries

Digitalised nineteenth-century newspapers available from the British Library. Courtesy of the British Library Board

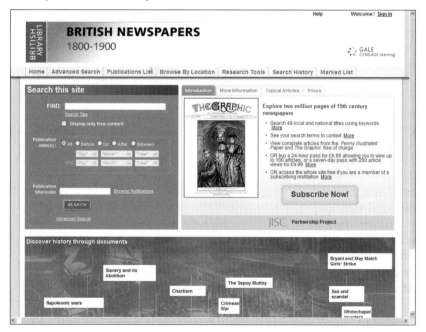

for London and across Britain, as well as various pamphlets and proclamations. Access is currently possible only through local authority and educational institutions with a subscription.

Subscription-based archives for several national titles are available online. *The Times* (1785–1985) is at **http://archive.timesonline.co.uk/tol/ archive**, but, like the British Library newspapers collections, can also be viewed for free through subscribing institutions, including many local libraries. Coverage for the paper from 1785–1820 is also carried at Footnote (**www.footnote.com**). Both the *Daily Express* and the *Daily Mirror* have twentieth-century archives available at **www.ukpressonline. co.uk**. Public access to the *Mirror* archive can only be gained up to 1980 (complete access is, however, offered to subscribing institutions), and twenty-first century editions of the *Sunday Express*, *Daily Star* and *Daily Star Sunday* are also available. Two other titles, *The Guardian* and *The Observer*, have also been digitised (1791–2003), and can be viewed at **http://archive.guardian.co.uk**.

The Scotsman Digital Archive (**http://archive.scotsman.com**) hosts copies of the *Scotsman* newspaper (1817–1950). Also for Scotland, an online *Guide to Scottish Newspapers Indexes* from the National Library of Scotland at **www.nls.uk/collections/newspapers/indexes/index.cfm** gives information on every Scottish title indexed, the years of coverage, and the locations of the indexes. Its *Word on the Street* project (**www.nls. uk/broadsides/index.html**) also depicts 1800 broadsides from across the country from 1650–1910.

In Ireland, the Irish Newspaper Archives (**www.irishnewsarchive. com**) has a truly impressive range of titles from across the island, including the *Irish Independent* and the *Donegal News*. In addition, another major all island resource is the *Irish Times* archive site (**www.irishtimes. com/premium/loginpage**). For the north, Eddie Connolly has extracted many stories and intimations from several Ulster based newspapers and placed them online at **http://freepages.genealogy.rootsweb.ancestry. com/~econnolly**. Nick Reddan's site at **http://members.iinet.net.au/ ~nickred/newspaper** is an all Ireland equivalent.

Ancestry provides a limited amount of newspaper material, including issues of *The Bristol Times and Mirror* from December 1897, London's *Daily Universal Register* from 1786 and 1787, and other papers covering Lancashire and Staffordshire, as well as a database of information extracted from the *Railway Gazette* from 1860–1930. WorldVitalRecords has a larger, rapidly expanding collection of English newspapers, with, at the time of writing, seventy titles represented, though coverage is again patchy. Its most extensive collection is for the *London Daily Mail*, with coverage from 1896–1923, though the availability of other titles is more fragmented, with for example, the *Daily Post* available for 1729, 1731, 1737–1738, 1739, and 1741–44. Another useful site carrying over a hundred English and British newspaper titles is the Newspaper Archive (**www.newspaperarchive.com**).

A free and often neglected resource is the *London Gazette*. The paper has been the official paper of record for the Government from the seventeenth century, carrying notices such as military medal awards, promotions, court appointment, civil honours, personal insolvencies and probate notices. Although most editions are keyword searchable, some editions from the seventeenth and eighteenth centuries were not scanned using optical character recognition technology, meaning that they must instead be browsed. The paper has sister titles in Edinburgh (from 1699) and Belfast (from 1922); all can be accessed at **www.gazettes-online.co.uk**. Following the Partition of Ireland a separate paper, the *Iris Ofigiúil*, was established to replace the all Ireland *Dublin Gazette*, but its archive can only be searched online from 2002 at **www.irisoifigiuil.ie**.

The *North of England Newspaper Archive* at **www.n-e-n-a.co.uk** is indexing and digitising titles for the region including the *Daily Gazette*, whist the Internet Library of Early Journals (**www.bodley.ox.ac.uk/ilej**) allows access to digitised editions of six eighteenth and nineteenth-century periodicals including the *Gentleman's Magazine* and *Notes and Queries*. Richard Heaton's Newspaper Collection at **http://tinyurl.com/3aaal9** further provides access to transcripts and extracts from just under 900 fully searchable Georgian and early Victorian Regional Newspapers, predominantly for Lancashire and the south of England.

Nobility and Gentry
If your blood is of the blue variety, Burke's Peerage and Gentry (**www.burkespeerage.com**) contains over a million names in its database connected to the British aristocracy. Although subscription based, there are some free resources available, such as guides to castles and houses across the country, as well as the various royal lineages of Britain.

The subscription-based Stirnet website (**www.stirnet.com**) provides pedigrees on many families from across the British Isles, whilst the similar but free The Peerage site (**www.thepeerage.com**) has many distinguished pedigrees compiled by New Zealand based Darrel Lundy.

Leigh Rayment's site at **http://leighrayment.com** provides further information on the British peerage, though without any pedigrees.

Debrett's (**www.debretts.com**) has a freely searchable biographical database of the top 25,000 'achievers' in Britain, and useful guides to such subjects as the Royal Family and British orders of chivalry. The official website for the British Monarchy is **www.royal.gov.uk**, which includes details on how to access the Royal Archives, whilst a list of the most important or senior Royal appointments since the fourteenth century can be found at **www.history.ac.uk/office**. The Directory of Royal Genealogical Data (**www3.dcs.hull.ac.uk/public/genealogy/royal/catalog.html**) contains the pedigrees of the British monarchy and other royal houses connected to it.

The Oxford Dictionary of National Biography (**www.oxforddnb.com**) contains over 57,000 biographies on the great and the good, as does Who's Who (**www.ukwhoswho.com**). Both are subscription based sites, though many libraries will provide free access. The Dictionary of Ulster Biography (**www.ulsterbiography.co.uk**) is a useful Northern Irish equivalent.

For English and Welsh heraldry, consult the College of Arms site (**www.college-of-arms.gov.uk**) for past editions of its newsletter available in PDF format. The Heraldry Society also has an online presence at **www.theheraldrysociety.com**. North of the border, heraldry matters are regulated by the Court of the Lord Lyon (**www.lyon-court.com**). Coats of arms have been digitised from the *Public Register of All Arms and Bearings* from 1672–1907 and made available at ScotlandsPeople. Many pre-1672 coats of arms, blazons and images can also be consulted at **www.heraldry-scotland.co.uk**.

For Ireland, visit **www.nli.ie/en/intro/heraldry-introduction.aspx** for entries between 1936 and 1980 in the *Registers of Grants of Arms* and an introduction to Irish heraldry, and **www.maproom.org/00/47/index.php** for several plates depicting Irish arms, as recorded in 1905.

If you are interested in obtaining items of silver with your family crest, My Family Silver (**www.myfamilysilver.com**) is well worth consulting. The sites's *Crestfinder* tool allows you to search through *Fairbairns Book of Crests*, and to search for an item carrying a particular design through the catalogues of some of the world's most famous auctioneering firms, such as Sotheby's and Christies.

Chapter Three

OCCUPATIONAL RECORDS

As well as creating a basic understanding of who our ancestors were and the locations in which they existed, it is also worthwhile pursuing the records of what they did for a living, to help us fully understand the daily struggles of their lives.

Often we will come across a trade name in an old record that completely throws us, but a handy site for enlightenment is **http:// rmhh.co.uk/occup**. There are many possible trades within which your forebears may have worked, and it would be impossible to list them all. Many online resources are detailed within the individual county sections of this book, but the following section may also help with some of the more specific occupations employing many across the nation.

The Armed Forces

Army

The United Kingdom has engaged in its fair share of wars across the centuries, and it is unlikely that your family does not have a military connection somewhere along the line, particularly in the major global conflicts of the twentieth century. One of the best sites covering the history of war in all its forms across the British Isles and beyond is the Military History Encyclopaedia on the Web (**www.historyofwar.org**). Equally useful is the British Battles site (**www.britishbattles.com**) and the Scots at War Trust (**www.scotsatwar.co.uk**).

Starting with the British Army, a list of museums in England and Wales is available from the Army Museums Ogilby Trust (**www. armymuseums.org.uk**), which also contains an extensive bibliography on resources for each regiment, whilst the National Army Museum (at **www.national-army-museum.ac.uk**) lists additional information. The Imperial War Museum's Collections Online site (**www.iwmcollections. org.uk**) provides many user guides in downloadable PDF format on how to research military ancestors, as well as several comprehensive online catalogues of its holdings. For those wishing to obtain copies of recent service records still held by the Ministry of Defence, the Veterans Agency (**www.veterans-uk.info**) has all the relevant information, as well as a guide to claiming medals. For replacement medals, consult **www.awardmedals.com**.

The Twentieth Century
Increasingly there is a great deal of First World War material being placed online. Possibly the most informative site on the history of the war itself is Chris Baker's exceptional website, The Long, Long Trail (**www.1914-1918.net**). It provides detailed accounts of the various regiments and battalions which fought, the campaigns engaged in, and some unusual genealogical gems, such as a page devoted to brothers known to have died on the same day. The site also carries war diaries, despatches, campaign maps and more, and is accompanied by the Great War Forum at **http://1914-1918.invisionzone.com/forums**, which covers just about every war topic that you may wish to discuss. The Western Front Association also has many handy background resources at **www.westernfrontassociation.com**, whilst the University of Oxford has a rich collection of material as submitted by members of the public at **www.thegreatwararchive.org**, including audio recordings of interviews, diaries, drawings, postcards, paintings, and other useful material that can help you to construct a sense of what it was like to be there. FirstWorldWar.com (**www.firstworldwar.com**) also provides a similarly themed multimedia guide to the war, whilst the BBC's *Remembrance* site, although no longer updated, still contains a great deal of commemorative material as supplied by the public at **www.bbc.co.uk/ remembrance**. Many contemporary documents concerning the Great War can also be accessed at **www.gwpda.org**.

About a third only of First World War soldiers' service records have survived, and have been digitised by Ancestry.co.uk. Held by TNA in series WO 363 and WO 364, the company has categorised them on its site as two collections, *British Army WW1 Service Records 1914–20* and *British Army WW1 Pensions 1914–20*. In fact, both contain service records, with the latter for soldiers who were discharged and who subsequently claimed for a pension. (It is worth noting that a very small number of misfiled service records for Boer War veterans are also found within the collection). Ancestry also has the *British Army Medal Rolls Index Cards 1914–20*, a collection of almost 5 million records listing soldiers and airmen who were entitled to receive a medal, which can help to identify campaigns within which your ancestor fought. The same cards are available at Documents Online, though only black and white copies of the fronts of the cards are supplied here, as opposed to Ancestry's colour scans of both sides, with the back of the cards sometimes revealing additionally useful information. On the plus side, Documents Online collection is better indexed, and has cards for women and civilian war workers. The Long Long Trail site has a handy page for interpreting the details on these cards at **www.1914-1918.net/ grandad/mic.htm**.

For the provision of soldiers' rolls of honour, the main genealogy vendors have all been heavily competing with each other, with the result that many of the key databases can now be sourced from several sources. Ancestry, along with FindmyPast, FamilyRelatives, and the Genealogist, has database versions of the *National Roll of the Great War*, *Soldiers Died in the Great War* and *De Ruvigny's Roll of Honour*, which can further help to identify soldiers who fought in the campaign. The same databases are also available at **www.military-genealogy.com**, where entries can be searched at 50p per entry, though with a minimum subscription of £5.

Additional First World War army resources at Documents Online include *Prisoner of War Interviews and Reports*, as recorded by the Committee on the Treatment of British Prisoners of War, service records for the Women's Army Auxiliary Corps, as well as the Victoria Cross registers (in fact from 1895 to 1944) and *Selected First World War and Army of Occupation War Diaries*, from 1914–22. If your ancestors were civilian prisoners of war, the Ruhleben Story (**http://ruhleben.tripod. com**) attempts to provide detailed biographical information on the 5500 British and Commonwealth citizens interned on the outskirts of Berlin during the conflict. The Red Cross (**www.icrc.org/web/eng/siteeng0. nsf/htmlall/archives?OpenDocument**) provides information on how to consult the society's archives for information on POWs, including an online application form.

For the Second World War, Documents Online has very little army material available, its only significant holding being the *Recommendations for Honours and Awards (1935–1990)*, which also contains details for RAF and RN personnel. Ancestry is however increasingly placing significant collections on its site, including the *UK Army Roll of Honour 1939–1945*, compiled from various War Office sources between 1944 and 1949, and the *UK British Army Prisoners of War 1939–1945* collection, with information on well over 100,000 POWs. The Genealogist equally hosts the Army Roll of Honour for World War Two, but also has records from the *Miscellaneous Foreign Returns, 1831–1964* (from TNA's RG 32 collection), which has notifications of deaths in Japanese and German POW camps, including names of those executed as prisoners.

A detailed timeline of the war is available at **www.worldwar-2.net**, whilst **www.secondworldwar.co.uk** offers some background information on the key players and some general statistics. General resource sites on the history of the war include two sites from military historian Paul Reed, being his D-Day site at **www.ddayancestors.com** and a site on the battle-fields and commemorations of the war at **www.ww2battlefields.info**, whilst Wartime Memories (**www.wartimememories.co.uk**) encourages the public to commemorate their military relatives' stories by making submissions to the site, as does *Keep the Memories Alive* site (**www. keepthememoriesalive.co.uk**). *Britain at War* is Ron Taylor's comprehensive site on the conflict which includes rolls of honour (including for British civilian war dead across the globe) and many essays on the various battles of the war. Although predominantly about the Second World War, it also covers the First World War and additional conflicts such as Suez. The Association of Jewish Ex-Servicemen and Women website (**www.ajex.org.uk/museum**) hosts a roll of honour for all Jewish service personnel to have lost their lives from 1939–60, with further information available at the Jewish Military Museum in London. A useful site providing an overview of the role of women throughout the war is located at **http://caber.open.ac.uk/schools/stanway/index. html**, whilst Northern Ireland's experience is outlined in detail at **www. secondworldwarni.org**.

Following the war, many people ended up doing National Service, and Alan Parkinson has produced an interesting site on his experience entitled National Service Memoirs (**www.nationalservicememoirs.co. uk**). Since 1945 the UK has also been involved in a series of conflicts and campaigns, raging from Korean and the Northern Irish Troubles to the Falklands and Iraq; for comprehensive information on these campaigns, and additional resources such as regimental histories and rolls of honour, visit **www.britains-smallwars.com**.

War memorials

The Commonwealth War Graves Commission (CWGC) hosts a database at **www.cwgc.org** of over 1.7 million British and Commonwealth service personnel who died during the two world wars, as well as 67,000 civilians who died between 1939 and 1945. A similar site is Pierre Vandervelden's *In Memory* (**www.inmemories.com**). Based in Belgium, Pierre has been valiantly photographing the various cemeteries and providing lists of all the Allied casualties within each, making it easy to see which other members of a regiment were buried alongside your ancestor, perhaps following the same military action. The *War Graves Photographic Project* (**www.twgpp.org**) is also working in tandem with the CWGC to provide images of every memorial from 1914 to the present day, whilst *In From the Cold* (**www.infromthecold.org**) is a sort of strays website, listing details of some 1500 further personnel not officially commemorated by the CWGC.

The Imperial War Museum has an inventory showing the locations of memorials across Britain for all wars at **www.ukniwm.org.uk** – whilst this does not contain individual soldiers' names at the time of writing, there are plans to add these in due course. Many First World War memorials are also listed at **www.roll-of-honour.com**, with details for British-based Royal Mail memorials further available at **http://catalogue. postalheritage.org.uk/dserve/bpma_docs/memorials.html**. The Scottish Military Research Group (**www.scottishmilitaryresearch.co.uk**) and the Scottish National War Memorial (**www.snwm.org**) can help north of the border.

Earlier campaigns

Prior to the First Word War, information was for a long time hard to find on the junior ranks without a visit to Kew, but in March 2010, FindmyPast commenced the mammoth release of Chelsea Pension records (held under WO 97 at TNA). Packaged as the *British Army Service Records 1760–1913* collection, this lists service records for soldiers pensioned out following their military service, most of whom were 'out-pensioners', i.e. not resident at the Royal Hospital at Chelsea itself. Following the complete upload of the collection in late 2011, the provider will then be turning its attention to the Irish equivalent of these records from the Royal Hospital Kilmainham.

A useful guide from TNA at **www.nationalarchives.gov.uk/military history/army/?WT.lp=mh-33483** explains where to direct your research efforts for both the lower ranks and officers. The latter are fairly well

John Henry Fry's service record from 1888; Barnstaple-born Fry served for just three days before being discharged. Crown copyright WO972843/23 reproduced courtesy of The National Archives and findmypast.co.uk recorded in annual guides such as Hart's Army List (established in 1839). A good selection of this and earlier lists dating back to 1798 is available at the FamilyRelatives site, providing information on an officer's career up to the date of each publication. The Internet Archive provides a useful regimental guide from 1901 at **www.archive.org/ details/cu31924030726503**, entitled *'The Regimental Records of the British Army: a Historical Resume Chronologically Arranged of Titles, Campaigns, Honours, Uniforms, Facings, Badges, Nicknames etc'.*

There are many sites dedicated to earlier campaigns – information on soldiers from all ranks involved in the Boer War is extensively recorded at **www.roll-of-honour.com/Boer**, with lists of medals awarded, the wounded, participating soldiers, POWs etc, and at **www.angloboerwar. com**. A guide by Rosemary Dixon-Smith on how to research ancestors in the war is also found at **www.genealogyworld.net/boer/tracing. html**. The *War Times Index* (**www.wartimesindex.co.uk**) is an archive of the Victorian wars with many names taken from despatches in the Gazette, the Times and other sources.

For the Napoleonic wars, the Peninsula Medal Roll is available at FindmyPast (1793–1814) and the Waterloo Medal Roll for 1815 (awarded to people as late as 1848), whilst a roll call of mainly officers present at Waterloo is available at FamilyRelatives (some NCOs are also listed). The Original Record website also carries many records for individual regiments.

For the history of the seventeenth-century Civil Wars in Britain visit **www.british-civil-wars.co.uk**, and if you are really confident that you have a connection as far back as the Hundred Years War, visit **www. medievalsoldier.org** for muster rolls, protection rolls and garrison rolls containing over 200,000 names between 1369 and 1453.

Finally, another site well worth visiting is that of the Army Children Archive (**www.archhistory.co.uk**), which chronicles how children raised in military families coped on a day to day existence.

Royal Air Force

Taking to the air, the Royal Air Force started initially as the Royal Flying Corps, the history of which is outlined from 1914–18 at **www.airwar1.org. uk**, with the site including some pilots' accounts of hostilities as well as information on the planes used. The Aerodrome (**www.theaerodrome. com**) is a site with a much wider remit, containing information on aces and aircraft from the various nations involved, including the UK.

Ancestry hosts the *Great Britain, Royal Aero Club Aviators' Certificates 1910–1950* collection which contains 28,000 index cards for pilots issued with licenses to fly. This includes the names and details of many who joined the RFC and the Royal Naval Air Service, as well as 33 out of 34 surviving photo albums containing images of many. Documents Online also has the service records of RAF officers, as well as members of the Women's Royal Air Force who served during the First World War. A Roll of Honour for airmen who have died whilst serving with the Fleet Air Arm can be searched at **www.fleetairarm.com/en-GB/rollofhonour. aspx**, mainly for the Second World War and onwards.

The RAF Museum, based at Cosford and Hendon, has a site at **www. rafmuseum.org.uk** with many useful resources, including download-able copies in PDF format of RAF Historical Society journals, details on the museum's resources, and online exhibitions such as *Lest We Forget*, which also includes a virtual *Book of Remembrance*. The museum's Navigator site (**http://navigator.rafmuseum.org**) has more detailed information on the collections, including many images. For a list of RAF squadron associations, and their contact details, visit **www.associations. rafinfo.org.uk/squadron.htm**, whilst a series of RAF lists from the 1920s can be consulted at FamilyRelatives, with information on all ranks from Air Marshal to Pilot Officer. If your ancestor fought in the Battle of Britain, it is well worth consulting **www.raf.mod.uk/bob1940** to view a Roll of Honour for the conflict and a set of daily reports pertaining to sorties between July and October 1940, whilst Air Ministry Combat Reports are available for the Second World War at Documents Online.

Many abbreviations found in RAF service records, and some RAF slang, can be decoded using **www.lancaster-archive.com/bc_abbreviations. htm**.

Royal Navy

For the senior service, there are several excellent resources which can be utilised. The Royal Navy itself has published a comprehensive time-line at **www.royalnavy.mod.uk/history/**, whilst the Naval-History.net site (**www.naval-history.net**) has an extensive collection of resources available on the history of its ships and personnel, including many rolls of honour. The site also contains many useful resources for the Navy's story from the First World War to the Falklands, including war diaries, a roll of honour for RN casualties from 1914–1920 and more.

Documents Online has several collections, including the *Registers of Seamen's Services* from 1853–1923, *Royal Naval Officers' Service Records* from 1756–1917, wills of Royal Naval Seamen from 1786–1882, *Women's Royal Naval Service Records* from 1917–1919, and also *Royal Naval Division Service Records* from 1914–19, detailing the reservist seamen who fought alongside the army in the trenches during the war (a database of WW1 Royal Naval Division casualties is also available from both FindmyPast and Ancestry). Earlier naval records exist on Documents Online in the form of logs from Royal Naval exploration voyages from 1757–1861. The site also has two collections for those with Royal Marines in their trees – *Royal Marines Service Records* from 1842–1936 and *Royal Marines: Selected Plymouth Attestations* from 1805–1848.

For earlier records of the navy prior to the twentieth century, the Naval Biographical database (**www.navylist.org**) contains entries of many officers from 1660 to 1870, but only in the form of an index, from which you can purchase a full report on the officer in question, after agreeing to a price from a supplied estimate, whilst a similar database of Commissioned Sea Officers from 1660–1815 is available at Family Relatives.com. Several Royal Naval lists can be viewed for free at the Internet Archive, containing details on officers, whilst The Genealogist also has thirteen lists from between 1822 and 1944 available. Paul Benyon has extracted many names from Navy lists from 1844–1879 and placed them online at **www.pbenyon1.plus.com/Nbd/Index.html**, with all ranks listed including carpenters, chaplains and more. TNA has a useful guide for researching ex-sailors who became Greenwich Pensioners at **www.nationalarchives.gov.uk/catalogue/RDLeaflet.asp?s LeafletID=41**.

To gain an idea about life in the navy in the early nineteenth century, and the battles of Trafalgar and the Nile, visit **www.nelsonsnavy.co.uk**, whilst an unusual site at **http://home.planet.nl/~pdavis** allows you to download a simulator of a three and two masted square rigged sailing ship from the period, HMS *Surprise*. TNA has a database listing everyone who served at Trafalgar at **www.nationalarchives.gov.uk/trafalgar ancestors**, with service details and additional biographical notes where known, whilst The Age of Nelson website (**www.ageofnelson.org**) may also be of help.

If your connection is with the submarine service, the Royal Naval Submarine Museum website (**www.rnsubmus.co.uk**) contains many photographic collections, an index of submarine losses, and a history of the service from its creation in 1901, as well as several online exhibitions.

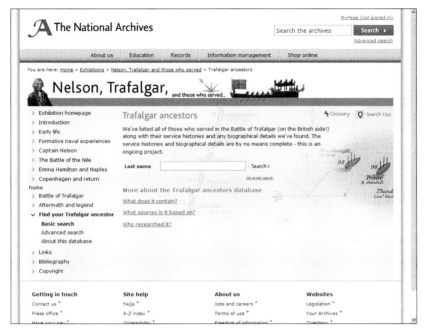

The National Archives database listing all those who fought at Trafalgar.
Courtesy of The National Archives

For a list of British coastguards as recorded in the censuses from 1841–1901, visit Stan Waight's list at **www.genuki.org.uk/big/Coastguards**, whilst for Irish coastguards visit the excellent Coastguards of Yesteryear site (**www.coastguardsofyesteryear.org**). Resources on Customs officials and their history can be found at **www.hm-waterguard.org.uk/People.htm**.

Merchant seamen

Shipping records for merchant seamen are held at archives across the British Isles and in many overseas countries such as Canada which traded heavily with the UK. Increasingly information on both the crews and the ships involved is finding its way on the net.

The National Maritime Museum at Greenwich has useful guides on how to research maritime ancestors at **www.nmm.ac.uk/contact**, along with details of its holdings. Several collections from TNA's Board of Trade records are available through Documents Online, including *Campaign Medals awarded to First World War Merchant Seamen, Medals*

Issued to Merchant Seamen (Second World War), *Second World War Merchant Shipping Movement Cards*, and *Indexes to Seamen's Names* from 1860–1867 (sourced from BT154/4-6 in TNA, a series which actually has further records from 1852–89, as yet not digitised). A list of convoy movements in the Second World War can be explored at **www.convoyweb.org.uk**, whilst for merchant seamen interned in Germany as prisoners of war in the First World War visit both **http://wanborough.ukuhost.co.uk/ POW/POW.htm** and **http://ruhleben.tripod.com**.

The Mariners site at **www.mariners-l.co.uk** has many resources including guides on how to research merchant navy ancestors, fishermen, shipping companies and more. Lloyd's Captains' Registers which give details on captains and mates serving on vessels whose details were transmitted to Lloyds have been indexed by the Guildhall Library and made available at **www.history.ac.uk/gh/capintro.htm** for the period from 1851–1911. Whilst many entries will need to be consulted at the library, some lists from 1800 are being digitised and made available at Google Books. The Crew List Index Project (**www.crewlist.org.uk**), which includes this and transcribed material from other sources, has made its database from 1861–1913 available on FindmyPast. For the north west of England, the Mighty Seas is a mighty project well worth consulting at **www.mightyseas.co.uk**.

There are several dedicated sites for Welsh mariner crew lists, including **www.welshmariners.org.uk**, **www.cardiffmariners.org.uk** and **www.swanseamariners.org.uk**. Almost 270,000 Irish mariners listed as working between 1918 and 1921 are indexed on the Irish Mariners website (**www.irishmariners.ie**), sourced from an index to the CR10 series of index cards held in Southampton Civic Archives. The Extracts from the Registers of Deceased Seamen at **http://freepages.genealogy. rootsweb.ancestry.com/~econnolly/register.html** indexes deaths from all over Ireland, the Shetland Islands and the Orkney Islands in the late nineteenth and early twentieth centuries. The Explore North website has many pages on the history of whaling, including some crew lists from Britain, at **http://explorenorth.com/whalers/index.html**.

The Maritime History Archive (**www.mun.ca/mha**) is focussed on Newfoundland, but has lots of British resources including a crew agreements database for 1863–1938 and an online catalogue. Going further back, a list of ships in the service of the East India Company is available at **www.eicships.info**, with information on the names of ship owners and captains included.

Workers' rights

The struggle for employees' rights was long fought, and greatly entangled with the fight for democracy itself. The Chartist Ancestors (**www. chartists.net**) explores the history of the mid nineteenth century Chartist movement, and includes lists of names, trials, uprisings and more, whilst the Working Class Movement Library (**www.wcml.org.uk**) covers many of the great strikes and campaigns, and lists holding within its archives at Salford. The Union History website (**www.unionhistory. info**) provides a trade union history timeline covering many industries over the last two centuries, as well as specialist sections on the General Strike of 1926, the Match Girls strike of 1888, the *Workers at War* project and more. The Trade Union Ancestors site has similar offerings at **www. unionancestors.co.uk**. For a list of offerings on the history of Scottish Labour at the National Library of Scotland visit **www.historycooperative. org/journals/lab/83/bell.html**.

Women were every bit as involved in the struggles for rights. TNA has a comprehensive site detailing the Suffragette movement at **www. learningcurve.gov.uk/britain1906to1918**, whilst an online exhibition using a series of case studies to demonstrate how women moved 'from the kitchen table to the conference table' is available at **www.political women.org.uk**.

Mining

On the mining front, the Coalmining History Resource Centre (**www. cmhrc.co.uk/site/home**) includes the *Royal Commission of Inquiry into Children's Employment 1842*, a national database of mining deaths in Great Britain, maps identifying the locations of mines and other resources. The University of Sunderland's North East England Mining Archive and Research Centre site (**www.neemarc.com**) includes a catalogue, leaflets on how to research your mining ancestors, and articles on various related subjects. The Durham Mining Museum (**www.dmm.org. uk/mindex.htm**) also carries a range of material, not just for Durham, but for surrounding counties, including accident reports, government reports, maps, a who's who, and more.

The history of women in the mines, including a list of women's deaths in the pits from 1851–1919 is provided by Leah Ryan and Ian Winstanley at **http://tinyurl.com/y6bgv77**, whilst Bill Riley's account of working life in the pits is online at **www.dmm-pitwork.org.uk**.

An overview of Welsh mining is provided at the Museum Wales site (**www.museumwales.ac.uk/en/bigpit**), and at the Welsh Mines Society (**www.welshmines.org**), with a list of mines in the Peak District in 1896 located at **www.pdmhs.com/MinesIndex1896Wales.asp**. For Scotland, the excellent Scottish Mining Website (**www.scottishmining.co.uk**) provides much useful context, as does The Hoods – History of a Coalmining Community at **www.hoodfamily.info/index.html** and many resources.

Communications

If your ancestors worked on the trains, the Railway Archive (**www.railwaysarchive.co.uk**) is a free online archive charting the development of Britain's railways, and includes accident reports and maps and other resources. Railscot (**www.railscot.co.uk**) also provides a history of railways in Britain, and as its title suggests, has a strong emphasis on Scotland, though also covers many companies in England and Wales. A description of archival holdings at the National Railways Museum at York and Shildon is available at **www.nrm.org.uk**. The Railway and Canal Historical Society (**www.rchs.org.uk**) also has detailed bibliographies of published literature relating to transport history from 2002–2007.

If you had ancestors living or working on Britain's canals, visit **www.canalmuseum.org.uk/collection/family-history.htm** for a useful guide on how to research their stories, and **www.virtualwaterways.co.uk** for the Virtual Waterways Archive Catalogue.

For the history and holdings of the British Postal Museum and Archive, as well as a downloadable guide on how to research postal family history, visit **www.postalheritage.org.uk**.

The Church

If your ancestor had a direct line to God, there are many useful online databases and sites to consult. The Church of England has a fully searchable archive catalogue at its Lambeth Palace site (**www.lambethpalacelibrary.org**), whilst a useful, though incomplete, site for researching Anglican ministers is the *Clergy of the Church of England Database* (**www.theclergydatabase.org.uk**), which contains information on members from 1540–1835. An important study detailing biographies on many Anglican cathedral-based clergy is the *Fasti Ecclesiae Anglicanae*, as drawn up by John Le Neve in 1716, and subsequently revised in 1854. A current project to re-evaluate the information in this important work, cathedral by cathedral, is being carried out by the Institute of Historical Research, which has made indexes available to their newly expanded edition at **www.history.ac.uk/resources/fasti**. Copies of the original editions by Le Neve are available to read and download from the Internet Archive, which also has Crockford's Clerical Directories from 1861 and 1868. Additional information on ministers recorded in Crockfords between 1858 and 1968 can be found at **www.crockford. org.uk**, though this is a subscription-based site with only a few limited free resources. Findmypast has also provided access to Kelly's Clergy List from 1896.

Biographies on Church of Scotland ministers are available in the *Fasti Ecclesiae Scoticanae* collection, first published in 1866, at the Internet Archive (**http://tinyurl.com/2ejhy92**), though Volume 5, covering Fife, Angus and Mearns, is fairly difficult to read having been poorly digitised. A much better digitisation of all the volumes is available at Ancestry. Entries for ministers in the United Presbyterian Church from 1733–1900 can also be found at **http://tinyurl.com/2dgrlzv**, whilst for Scottish Episcopal Clergy visit Google Books at **http://tinyurl.com/ 2cch5pn**.

For nonconformist ancestors, the University of Manchester hosts a site for Methodist records at **www.library.manchester.ac.uk/special collections/collections/methodist**, including an online virtual library, whilst the Wesley Historical Society has a *Dictionary of Methodism in Britain and Ireland* at **http://dmbi.wesleyhistoricalsociety.org.uk**. For Quakers, the Society of Friends has a library catalogue at **www.quaker. org.uk/library**, whilst the former English Presbyterian Church and Congregational Church, now the United Reform Church, has a limited site at **www.urc.org.uk/about/history_society/history_soc/history_soc**. The *Surman Index* of Congregational ministers from the mid seventeenth century to 1972 is also available online at **http://surman.english.qmul. ac.uk,** whilst a series of obituaries for ministers of the Unitarian Church from 1900–1004 is available at **www.unitariansocieties.org.uk/historical/ ministerobit.html**. A further resource for Unitarian ministers is the *Dictionary of Unitarian and Unitarian Biography* at **www25.uua.org/uuhs/ duub**. The Salvation Army's International Heritage Centre in London has many historical resources at **www2.salvationarmy.org.uk/history**.

For Roman Catholics, the Catholic Record Society site (**www. catholic-history.org.uk/crs**) contains an index of articles for both its 'Recusant History' series and its 'Records Series', as well as details of other published monographs. The site also provides links to various Catholic history societies across England, including the Catholic Family History Society at **www.catholic-history.org.uk/cfhs/index.htm**. For Scotland visit **www.scottishcatholicarchives.org.uk**.

The main gateway for records concerning missionaries is the Mundus website (**www.mundus.ac.uk**), which lists over 400 separate collections. The University of Southern California's Internet Mission Photography Archive (**http://digitallibrary.usc.edu/impa**) is also well worth consulting, as is the catalogue of holdings for the School of Oriental and African Studies (**http://squirrel.soas.ac.uk/dserve**).

The Law
If you have policemen in the family tree, the relevant local force's archive can be identified through a guide written by Ian Bridgeman and Clive Emsley available at **www.open.ac.uk/Arts/history/policing/police-archives-guide/index.html**, though as it was written in 2006 some contact details may be out of date. The Police History Society has additional details at **www.policehistorysociety.co.uk**, with links to many genealogically useful sites such as the Police Roll of Honour (also accessible at **www.policememorial.org.uk**) and various museums across the country. The Open University has many holdings listed on its Police Collections page (**http://library.open.ac.uk/find/specialcol/index.cfm?id=7158**). A site for those collecting police memorabilia exists at **www.constabulary.com**, which contains some discussion on the history of the force, as well as many photos.

Of course, your ancestors may well have strayed over to the dark side, or have been severely punished for a crime which would today seem trivial. The Ancestry website has digitised 279 English and Welsh criminal registers from 1791–1882 as part of its World Archives Project. The registers were sourced from the HO26 and HO27 Home Office collections at TNA and provide information about the individuals charged, their trial and sentence, if convicted, or any other outcome. The Old Bailey website (**www.oldbaileyonline.org**) has also made documents freely available from almost 200,000 trials carried out at the London court from 1674–1913, as well as an *Ordinary of Newgate's Accounts*, which provides information on the lives and deaths of convicts at Tyburn from 1692–1772. The stories of some of the most notable executed convicts in Britain during the eighteenth and nineteenth centuries are also available via the Newgate calendar at **www.exclassics.com/newgate/ngintro.htm**. State sponsored execution is also dealt with at **www.capitalpunishmentuk.org**, which not only provides a list of those executed across the British Isles, but also a history of the death penalty itself.

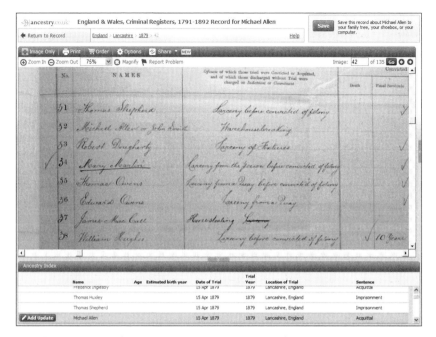

Searching the English and Welsh criminal registers from 1791–1888. Courtesy of Ancestry.co.uk

For details on prisoners in other British prisons, consult **www. blacksheepindex.co.uk** and **www.blacksheepancestors.com/uk**. The Victorian Crime and Punishment site at **http://vcp.e2bn.org** also provides a searchable database of prisoners from the nineteenth century for the UK as well as individual case studies. For Welsh criminals, consult the National Library of Wales' Crime and Punishment database at **www.llgc.org.uk/sesiwn_fawr/index_s.htm**, which features records extracted from the gaol files of the Court of Great Sessions in Wales from 1730–1830.

Theatrical

If your ancestors once trod the boards for a living then the Theatre Database (**www.theatredatabase.com**) may be of use, charting performances and performers from ancient times to the twentieth century. *The Stage* magazine (**www.thestage.co.uk**) has an online subscription-based archive covering 125 years of theatrical history, with a 24 hour pass costing £5, whilst Footlight Notes (**http://footlightnotes.tripod.com**) is an online magazine specifically covering performance history. The East London Theatre Archive is another impressive database available at **www.elta-project.org**.

Alternatively, your ancestors may have been travelling performers. The University of Sheffield's National Fairground Archive (**www.nfa. dept.shef.ac.uk**) includes a history of fairgrounds, articles, galleries, and a guide to using the Sheffield-based archive itself, whilst the Circus Historical Society site (**www.circushistory.org**) includes many genealogical resources, such as route books, censuses and directories. The UK Fairground Ancestors site (**www.members.shaw.ca/pauline 777/TravellersUK.html**) includes biographies of some of the more prominent fairground families.

On the musical front, the Arts and Humanities Research Council has a database of musical concert programmes in the UK and Ireland at **www.concertprogrammes.org.uk**.

Medical

Accessing medical records can often be tricky, with individual local authorities operating different closure periods. TNA's Hospital Records Database (**www.nationalarchives.gov.uk/hospitalrecords**) can help locate many records held in archives across the country. If this does not list your hospital, try the website of your local county records office or university archive.

In 1948 the principle provider of today's health care arrived in the form of the National Health Service. The BBC has a history of the service at **www.bbc.co.uk/archive/nhs**, whilst in Scotland, there is coverage at **www.60yearsofnhsscotland.co.uk**.

The Rossbret UK Institutions website (**www.institutions.org.uk**) has information on a variety of hospitals, asylums, workhouses, orphanages ands almshouses. If your ancestor was placed within a workhouse ('poorhouse' in Scotland), the website to check for the location of records is **www.workhouses.org.uk**, whilst the location of asylums can also be found through **www.countyasylums.com**.

Several medical directories and gazetteers are available on both Ancestry and FamilyRelatives. The catalogue for Royal College of Surgeons in England (established in 1800) can be consulted at **www. rcseng.ac.uk/library**, whilst the Scottish equivalent, the Royal College of Surgeons of Edinburgh (established 1505) has a similar site at **www.rcsed.ac.uk/site/355/default.aspx**. For surgeons and physicians, licenses to practice issued by the Archbishop of Canterbury between

1580 and 1775 are indexed at **www.lambethpalacelibrary.org/files/ Medical_Licences.pdf**. The Royal College of Physicians' library has an online catalogue at **www.rcplondon.ac.uk/library**, as does its Scottish equivalent (**www.rcpe.ac.uk/library/index.php**), with a history of the establishment. The Ulster Medical Society Archives (**www.ums.ac.uk**) has transcripts of various histories of medicine in Ulster from 1934 and 1967, whilst the ScotlandsPlaces site (**www.scotlandsplaces.gov.uk**) carries Medical Officers of Health Reports for Scotland from 1895. For information on researching midwives visit **www.rcm.org.uk**.

Information concerning St. John's Ambulance's history and archive can be found at **www.sja.org.uk,** whilst resources for the British Red Cross can be found at **www.redcross.org.uk/standard.asp?id=2623.**

Business
The locations of many records for business can be sourced from the National Register of Archives (see p. 8), and its Scottish equivalent, the National Register of Archives for Scotland (**www.nas.gov.uk/ onlineregister**). The *London Gazette,* and its Belfast and Edinburgh

The National Register of Archives database. Courtesy of The National Archives

counterparts (see p. 36), is always worth examining for notices of appointments of partners, mergers, dissolutions, retirements and even bankruptcies. Many business records will also be sourced locally in local authority and university-based archives.

Chapter Four

ENGLAND

As well as general resources for England, there are a great many locally-based websites that can assist your research, including archives, libraries, family history societies, and locally created history and genealogy resource sites. The following chapter lists some of the more useful on a county by county basis.

Bedfordshire

The Bedfordshire Libraries website hosts a town by town records resource guide at **http://tinyurl.com/y8dktam**, with gazetteer descriptions from 1586 and 1866–69 also available at **www.genoot.com/eng/bdf/index.html**.

Hugh Winters' Bedfordshire Surnames List (**http://homepages.ihug.co.nz/~hughw/bedf.html**) contains contact details for researchers with specific surname interests, whilst a look-up Exchange site exists at **http://williamsgwynfa.tripod.com/bedfordshirelookupexchange**. The county is particularly well served with regard to monumental inscriptions, with almost 200,000 headstones from 657 burial grounds (including some for Norfolk) recorded at the pay-per-view **www.memorialinscriptions. org.uk** site. Each entry costs £4-£7 to access, and in return you receive details of the inscription, a photo and further details of the relevant church.

A site for the Anglican parish church of All Saints in Renhold is hosted at **www.all-saints-church-renhold.org**, which includes a list of the clergy from 1229, a village map, and baptismal, marriage and burials registers transcriptions from 1602–1812, as well as banns from 1754–1812. The history of Ampthill is recorded at **www.ampthill.info/**

page10.htm, whilst for Turvey a useful site is **http://turvey.homestead. com**, which includes a list of inhabitants from the village in 1551 and transcripts from several nineteenth-century post office directories.

Great Barford parish register transcriptions from 1813 are available at Steve Gibb's website at **www.sgibbs1.freeserve.co.uk/gtbarford**, as well as several census returns and electoral register lists, whilst at **www.leighton-linslade.com** you can access information on the town of Leighton-Linslade and the villages of Billington, Eggington, Heath and Reach, and Stanbridge – the site also contains an index to events in the area during the 1860s, as recorded in the *Leighton Buzzard Observer*.

A gaol register index database from 1801–1901 has been placed at **http://apps.bedfordshire.gov.uk/grd** by the county archive, with details of 35,000 cases, providing the criminal's name, age, colour of hair, height, crime committed, trial dates, and details of punishment if convicted. A separate project at **www.schools.bedfordshire.gov.uk/gaol** provides Bedford Gaol's history from 1801–1877. If your ancestors were more law abiding, you may find them in local poll books for 1722 at **www.rabancourt.co.uk/abacus/p1722h.html** and from 1784 at **www. rabancourt.co.uk/abacus/p1784h.html**, both transcribed by Dr John Dawson.

For the history of Bedfordshire's lace industry visit **www.sandbenders. demon.co.uk/bobbinlace/history.htm**.

Berkshire

The Royal County of Berkshire website (**www.berkshirehistory.com**) contains many useful articles and resources on the area's history, such as a study of the Great Riot of 1327 in Abingdon, as well as information on folklore, historic buildings and more. Pigot's Directory for the county in 1830 is transcribed and available at **http://tinyurl.com/ydh64f3**. Local civil records indexes can be accessed at **www.BerkshireBMD.org.uk**.

An index to Bishop's Transcripts for Appleford (1563–1835) and parish registers for the baptismal register from Lambourne (1560–1837) have both been made available at **www.pbenyon1.plus.com/PR_Index. html**, whilst register transcriptions for Cumnor are available at **www. bodley.ox.ac.uk/external/cumnor**, which also includes monumental inscriptions for St. Michaels' Churchyard and a 'Who Was Who' for the parish for the period 1450–1900. Further Bishops' Transcripts for Cookham from 1607–1635 can be found at **http://tinyurl.com/y92zdo4**.

The parish of Bucklebury is well served at **http://home.btconnect. com/buckleburyweb/history.htm**, whilst Wraysbury's past is explored at **www.wraysbury.net/history.htm**, with the site providing a handy historic timeline and village photos. For Faringdon, **www.faringdon. org/hyhistory1.htm** hosts resources for the village's war memorial, the United Reform Church, the Civil War, Coles Pits and more. Beenham village's history is dealt with at **www.beenhamonline.org/history.htm**, whilst for Cox Green, in the parish of Bray, a series of census strays of parishioners born elsewhere in the country and enumerated between 1841–91 is listed at **www.heuristics-ltd.co.uk/heritage/genealogy/strays/ straysintro.htm**. A bibliography of useful resources for Newbury can be found at **www.burrell-wood.org.uk/LHist/index.htm**.

One of the more interesting sites from the county is the Hungerford Virtual Museum at **www.hungerfordvirtualmuseum.co.uk**, with many transcribed resources in the Archive section such as lists of quit rents, constables' accounts, maps and plans, and considerably more. The Reading History Trail at **http://atschool.eduweb.co.uk/radstock/rht** is also well worth a visit, whilst a generic project for the heritage of Bracknell Forest area is located at **www.bfheritage.org.uk**.

An index for the *Windsor and Eton Express* newspaper from 1826–1842 is available at **http://tinyurl.com/yz8q3zz**, which contains about 13,000 names. The Wiltshire and Berkshire Canal Trust site at **www.wbct. org.uk/history** has many articles extracted from newspapers as far back as 1800, and documents concerning legislation surrounding the canals.

The University of Reading's Museum of English Rural Life website at **www.reading.ac.uk/merl/collections/merl-collections.aspx** hosts several online databases. These include a useful *Bibliography of British and Irish Rural History* and an online exhibition linked to the museum's *Digitisation of Countryside Images* project, containing a sample of 300 photographs. The university's Research Centre for Evacuee and War Child Studies (ResCEW) also has an online presence at **www.reading. ac.uk/education/partners/ioe-evacuees-archive.aspx**.

And if you fancy something to accompany your tea break, read about the history of biscuit making in Reading by Huntley and Palmers at **www.huntleyandpalmers.org.uk**.

Buckinghamshire

The Milton Keynes Heritage Association website at **www.mkheritage. co.uk** is your first stop for research into Buckinghamshire ancestry. It not only acts as a gateway to many useful sites, from the Bletchley Park Trust to the Open University Archive, but also hosts dedicated pages for many organisations across the county, including the Buckingham Canal Society and The Old Stratford Remembered Group. The Living Archives project (**www.livingarchive.org.uk/docs/archivestories.html**) also carries interesting essays on the history of Milton Keynes, including stories about wartime evacuees, and the birth of the city.

A Buckinghamshire land owners list from 1873 can be consulted at **www.burrell-wood.org.uk/LHist/index.htm**, detailing everyone who owned more than an acre of land.

A detailed one place study site for the parish of Wing in the Vale of Aylesbury is available at **www.wing-ops.org.uk**, including parish record transcriptions and strays, muster rolls, gazetteer entries, directories and even Sun Insurance records. A website containing a database of instances of the surname 'Roads', as well as surnames appearing in one-place studies of the villages of Waddesdon, Grendon Underwood and Wotton Underwood, is available at **http://wc.rootsweb.ancestry.com/ cgi-bin/igm.cgi?db=hohrer** – the site contains both a simple search and advanced search screen which allows you to search for particular vital events. If your ancestor was from Tingewick, you will find a welcome page on resources for the village at **http://freepages.genealogy.rootsweb. ancestry.com/~tingewick/index.htm**. A fantastic collection of church photographs from across the county can also be found at **www. countyviews.com/bucks/church.htm**.

Monumental inscriptions for St Michael's Church in Hornton can be found at **http://met.open.ac.uk/genuki/big/eng/BKM/Horton/MIs.html**, and for the Church of All Saints at Calverton at **www.xor.org.uk/ calverton/crj97/crj_20.htm**.

Cambridgeshire (and Isle of Ely)
The modern East Anglian county of Cambridgeshire is consider-ably larger today than its historic equivalent, including the Isle of Ely (formerly a county palatine in itself), the old county of Huntingdonshire and the borough of Peterborough (see p. 84).

Cambridgeshire Council is making its local statutory indexes available online from 1837–2002 via its CAMDEX service at **www. cambridgeshire.gov.uk/community/BMD/camdex**. Whilst these are not yet complete, the site does helpfully list exactly what is and what is not available. Following successful searches, the records can then be ordered and paid for online.

Ancestry and FindmyPast host Cambridgeshire parish register records, as does the Genealogist website in its *Parish Records* collections, although the records for St Michael's of Cambridge are curiously hidden away within the *Directories* section, under the title of *1538–1837 Cambridge BMD Directory*.

The Cambridgeshire Community Archives Network (**www.ccan. co.uk**) hosts many images, documents and historic accounts compiled by members of the public. If you are looking for famous folk to have come from the county, visit **www.rootsweb.ancestry.com/~engcam/ famspple.htm**.

Cambridgeshire FHS (**www.cfhs.org.uk**) provides several useful databases online, including baptisms and burial indexes from 1801–37, a strays index, an index to poor law papers, indexes for the 1841 and 1851 censuses for the county and an 1891 census index for Cambridge St Andrew the Less. The site also offers a Victoria gold rush emigration database listing surname, forename, and year of birth of many who emigrated from the county – unfortunately the original database is now missing and so no further details can be given. A look-up exchange for records within the county can also be consulted at **www.links.org/**

The one place study of Soham. Courtesy of Soham Roots, Soham, Cambridgeshire

Lookups/Cambs/, with various volunteers willing to do look-ups for records such as poll books for the county from 1780, 1802 and 1831.

Parish and census indexes for Carlton-cum-Willingham can be found within the history section at **www.carlton-cambridgeshire.org.uk**, whilst a series of websites by Steve Odell provides similar material for the village of Arrington (**www.arrington.org.uk**), as well as photos for the village and Croydon, Orwell and Wimpole at **www.steve.odell.dsl.pipex.com**. Monumental inscriptions, census entries and rolls of honour for Foxton can be found in the genealogy section at **www.foxtoncambs.info**, whilst the site's history page has several gazetteer and directory descriptions of the village from 1794, 1851 and 1929. The village of Milton is similarly served at **www.miltonvillage.org.uk/opus129.html** and Littleport at **http://littleportsociety.org.uk/genealogy.html**. For essays on the history of Little Thetford, visit **http://ow.ly/17Uwg**.

The Fenstanton Village site (**www.fenstanton-village.co.uk**) offers a Master Genealogical Index to various vital events and census records, but you must first register with the site, after which you will be e-mailed a link to a PDF file containing the information. The index is surname-based only, and you will need to purchase a book from the site entitled *Beyond Yesterday – A History of Fenstanton* by Jack Dady (£9.95), after which you are then entitled to ask for unlimited free look-ups for the original documents contained in the index.

Probably the best Cambridgeshire local history site is that for the village of Soham at **www.sohamroots.co.uk**, with carries a local history and a great deal of folklore to keep you busy for hours. Extracts from the *Soham Chronicle* (1787–1899) have been provided at **http://homepage.ntlworld.com/s.walker10/soham_chronicle%20main.htm**, whilst Soham Grammar school's site at **www.sohamgrammar.org.uk** has a roll of honour for former pupils who fell in the two worlds wars.

If your ancestors came from the Cambridgeshire Fens, **http://contueor.com/wisbech** has links to a variety of resources for parishes in the area (as well as for parts of Norfolk and Lincolnshire). If from the village of Prickwillow you should visit **www.rootsweb.com/~engcam/Prickwillow/Pwillow.htm** for a brief history, a list of inhabitants from 1929 and images from the village war memorial. For Chaterris, there is a genealogy guestbook at **http://resources.rootsweb.com/~guestbook/cgi-bin/public_guestbook.cgi?gb=3789&action=view** where you can post messages to seek connections with relatives.

Other miscellaneous sites of interest for the county include the Churches of Cambridgeshire site at **www.druidic.org/camchurch/links**.

htm, and a site on the history of cholera in Ely at **www.rootsweb. ancestry.com/~engcam/cholera.htm**. Finally, a list of graduates from Cambridge University is available on Ancestry.

Cheshire
One of four English marches counties on the Welsh border, the historic county of Cheshire was reorganised into two separate authorities on April 1st 2009 (Cheshire East, and Cheshire West & Chester). Cheshire and Chester Archives (**www.cheshire.gov.uk/recoff**) continues to work for both authorities, holding many useful online resources, including historical photos from the county, a catalogue of the archive's holdings, a wills database with over 130,000 wills confirmed from 1492–1940, tithe maps in use during the mid nineteenth century, and more.

Eight directories for the county from 1789–1910 can be found transcribed at **http://cheshiredirectories.manuscripteye.com/index.htm**, whilst three further directories for Stockport and its surrounding districts from 1902, 1907 and 1910 are available at **http://interactive.stockport. gov.uk/Heritage/Directories**. This site also hosts a list of Stockport-based Methodists from January 1st 1794 (most other links on the page are broken). A map of Cheshire from circa 1850 is available at **www. jlb2005.plus.com/wales/tallis/maps/chs.htm**.

More generally, *A Scrapbook of Cheshire* (**www.thornber.org**) contains 959 photographs and commentary on 112 historic sites around the county. The detail for each parish varies, from a simple description of the church at Acton to a genealogical pedigree for the Downes family from the wonderfully named village of Pott Shrigley. Photographs of over 450 churches in the county are located at **www.moston.org/ churches.html**.

Indexes for locally registered civil registration records can be found at **www.cheshirebmd.org.uk**, whilst a look-up exchange exists at **www.rootsweb.ancestry.com/~engchs2**. The FamilySearch Record Search pilot website has made a great deal of material freely available, including bishops transcripts for the county's churches (1598–1900), non-conformist records (1671–1900), parish registers (1538–2000), school records (1796–1950) and registers of electors (1842–1900), whilst a separate Cheshire Parish Register Project has transcripts for records from 21 parishes at **www.csc.liv.ac.uk/~cprdb**.

Monumental inscriptions for Middlewich Cemetery are available at **http://users.domaindlx.com/Magicmark/MidCem/Book_12D2list.asp**, whilst those for twenty further parishes can also be found at **www. wishful-thinking.org.uk/genuki/CHS**. A comprehensive list of all known monumental inscriptions projects that have been carried out in the county is available through the main Family History Society of Cheshire website (**www.fhsc.org.uk**), whilst the society's Crewe-based branch has transcribed two books online at **www.scfhs.org.uk** which detail the heraldic visitations to the county in 1580 and 1613.

Parish resources for Kelsall's two churches (Methodist and Anglican) are at **www.the-dicksons.org/Kelsall/kelsall/parish.htm**, pages concerning the villages of Disley, Lyme Handley, Taxal and Whaley Bridge (Yeardsley cum Whaley) at **www.disley.net**, with resources including census, wills, rolls of honour and strays transcriptions, and a history of Holmes Chapel is available at **http://alancheshire.tripod.com/index-11. html**. St. Anne's in Sale is well served by a brilliant website at **www. stannesale.bravehost.com** which contains vestry minutes transcriptions, a roll of honour, war memorial transcriptions, list of benefactors, and considerably more. Tatton manor is explored at **http://tattonpark. cheshirealan.org.uk**, providing information not only on the manorial lords of the Tatton Park estate, but the many staff members who worked there. The county town of Chester is also well explored at **www. chesterwalls.info**.

The history of Cheshire's police is detailed at the county's Museum of Policing site at **www.museumofpolicingincheshire.org.uk**. It includes an online catalogue of the museum's holdings and an online application form for research that can be done by the staff. A register of prisoners held at Chester Gaol between 1810–1816 is available at **www.rootsweb. ancestry.com/~engchs/prison.html**. And if you are wondering who might have been responsible for the Dutch courage at the heart of many incidents, visit **http://members.tripod.com/%7EAlanCheshire/index-36. html** to explore a list of brewers from the county.

Cornwall

The *Cornwall Online Parish Clerks* website at **www.cornwall-opc.org** provides free access to genealogical information for all parishes within the county. As well as a Resources page with articles on various subjects of local interest, and a map of the county identifying the location of individual parishes, the site also has a detailed parish list, with each parish having its own dedicated website page and 'clerk' to co-ordinate the research for that location. Some have placed full transcriptions or relevant records online, whilst others elect to do free look-ups instead via e-mail. A consolidated *Search Database* exists on the site for all uploaded records, and can be searched for parish register and civil registration records, as well as other materials.

The *Cornwall Parish Register Index* at **www.cornwalleng.com** also carries a searchable database and a detailed parish map showing the parochial boundaries. The St Keverne Local History Society site at **www.st-keverne.com/history/records** hosts various databases for baptisms, marriages and burials, census records, quarter sessions records, old family deeds and leases, and other sets for the parish, whilst Althea Barker's site at **http://freepages.genealogy.rootsweb.com/ ~althea/index.html** has records for Breage and Godolphin, including bastardy bonds, the 1522 military survey, a 1569 muster roll, and probate records.

The *Cornish Database* site at **http://webs.lanset.com/azazella/cornish_ database.html** hosts wills abstracts for the county from 1582–1869, manorial records for Ludgvan Lese manor, and has dedicated parish sites for Morvah, Gwithian and Penwith. For West Penwith, Rick and Mary Parsons' site at **http://west-penwith.org.uk** carries many interesting items on the local dialect, Masonic lodges, maps, mines, manors, public houses, Quakers, and more.

For burial records, the Born Cornwall, Died… site at **http://free pages.genealogy.rootsweb.com/~chrisu/index.htm** carries a guide to cemeteries throughout the county, including photographs and a database of monumental inscriptions. A burial index for St Agnes from 1790–99 can also be found at **http://home.freeuk.com/lesley.morgan/ StAgnes_1790s_burials.htm**. Burials for St Mewan, as well as newspaper transcriptions, maps and the histories of many local families, can be found at **http://freepages.genealogy.rootsweb.ancestry.com/ ~boneplace/stmewan/contents.html**.

The *Cornwall Online Census Project* at **http://freepages.genealogy. rootsweb.ancestry.com/~kayhin/cocp.html** has transcriptions for the whole county for all censuses from 1841–1901. Kelly's Directory from 1873 for the parish of St. Minver is also online at **www.stminveropc. fsworld.co.uk/Dir_Kelly_1873.htm**, whilst a list of residents in Redruth from the 1910 edition is available at **www.connorsgenealogy.com/ Cornwall**.

An interactive gazetteer map of Cornwall is at **www.cornwall-calling.co.uk/map-cornwall-gazetteer.htm**, and further gazetteers at **www.oldcornwall.org**, as well as old postcards, church histories, glossaries of old Cornish words and a discussion forum. Newspaper transcriptions from the *West Briton and Cornwall Advertiser* from 1836–1887 are located at **http://freepages.genealogy.rootsweb.ancestry.com/~wbritonad**.

The Geevor Tin Mine Museum site (**www.geevor.com/index.php? page=38**) lists many mining history resources, whilst the Stone and Quarrymen of the West Country site at **http://freepages.genealogy. rootsweb.ancestry.com/~stonemen** names masons, quarrymen, builders, carpenters and other related occupations from both Cornwall and neighbouring Devon.

For Devon and Cornwall police, the force's heritage site at **www. policeheritagecentre.co.uk** contains a potted history, an online virtual museum and museum catalogues.

Finally, the Scilly Isles Museum at **www.iosmuseum.org** hosts short family history and archaeology sections which may help.

Cumberland

The Cumbria Family History Society (**www.cumbriafhs.com**) has a free discussion forum which can help those with roots in the historic county of Cumberland. The Past Presented site (**www.pastpresented.info/ index.htm**) carries a diverse range of material from transcriptions of eighteenth century newspapers, essays on the Great Storms of 1795–96, an Allonby news index, Lucinda's Tour of the Lake District in 1781, views around Millom steelworks from 1968, and several essays about Whitehaven. A guide to Cumbrian manorial records has been produced by the University of Lancaster and can be found at **www.lancs.ac.uk/ fass/projects/manorialrecords/index.htm**.

Cumberland Roots (**www.cumberlandroots.co.uk**) hosts records indexes and transcriptions sourced from both parish registers and bishops transcripts for fifteen separate parishes. Cumbrian Genealogy (**www.btinternet.com/~grigg**) carries additional resources from publications produced by the Parish Register Section of the Cumberland and Westmorland Antiquarian and Archaeological Society, with entries from various parishes indexed alphabetically by surname. The site also has census indexes for 1851 (by both names and place), and lists of inhabitants from several local county directories. Further records can be found at **www.edenlinks.co.uk/EDENLINKS.HTM** including parish register entries for Bolton, Brigham, Crosscanonby, Crosthwaite, Dean, Kirklinton, Lampkugh, and Mosser, as well as Land Tax assessments from 1764, whilst the Cumberland and Westmorland Archives site (**www.cumberlandarchives.co.uk**) has further church records, and transcribed materials such as 'An Abstract of the Sufferings of the People Called Quakers' from 1650–1666.

Photos of gravestones from across Cumberland are available at **www. stevebulman.f9.co.uk/cumbria/frames_home.html**, along with other historic county-sourced photographs and other resources, such as Jollie's Guide of 1811, lists of shipping which worked out of Cumberland, a *Carlisle Index*, and biographical entries for many of the county's more famous people. Additional historic photos can be found at the Cumbria Images Collection site at **http://cumbriaimagebank.org.uk/ index.php**.

Historic newspaper intimations concerning births, baptisms, marriages and deaths have been made available at **http://cumberlandbirthmarriage deaths.yolasite.com**, whilst the Cumberland and Westmorland Newspaper Transcriptions site at **www.cultrans.com** carries additional newspaper transcriptions, as well as monumental inscriptions for Egremont Cemetery and several burial grounds in Whitehaven. At **www. cumberlandhistory.co.uk** you can also view a handful of old issues of the *West Cumberland Times* from 1895–1930 and the *Cumberland Lake District Life* magazine from 1970–1979.

Derbyshire

Derbyshire has many exceptional resource sites online. The Yesterdays Journey project at **http://homepages.rootsweb.ancestry.com/~spire/ Yesterday/index.htm** carries a great deal of useful genealogical material, including apprenticeship records, bastardy papers, coroners' records, cemetery records, wills and more. Three other sites effectively carve the county up into projects for their respective regions. The South Derbyshire Genealogy Pages at **http://freepages.genealogy.rootsweb. ancestry.com/~brett/sdindex.htm** contain transcriptions of the 1841 census and 1662 hearth tax assessments for parishes in the region, as well as various nineteenth century trade directory descriptions for Repton and Grisley. Jayne's North East Derbyshire site at **http:// homepages.rootsweb.ancestry.com/~spire/index.htm** is a gateway for resources for parishes within Scarsdale hundred, whilst the North West Derbyshire Sources site at **http://freepages.genealogy.rootsweb.ancestry. com/~dusk** provides additional resources for its region, including jury lists and hearth tax assessments.

A transcription of White's 1857 Directory can be accessed at **www. n.f.wilson.btinternet.co.uk**, whilst Derbyshire's Parishes 1811 (**http:// dspace.dial.pipex.com/town/terrace/pd65/dby/index.htm**) provides a description for each parish in the county that year as noted in David Peter Davies' book *History of Derbyshire*. Kelly's Directory for 1891 can also be accessed at **www.andrewspages.dial.pipex.com/dby/kelly/ index.htm**.

General guides for both Derbyshire and the Peak District exist at **www.buxtononline.net** and **www.derbyshireheritage.co.uk**, whilst over 2000 photos of locations across the county can be viewed at **www. derbyphotos.co.uk**.

An account of the Pentrich Rebellion of 1817 is found online at **www.pentrichrebellion.co.uk** including a list of those who were trans-ported to Australia and a play transcript about the event. Records from 1600–1900 for the greater Wirksworth and Matlock are available at **www.wirksworth.org.uk**. The site is difficult to navigate, but is packed with useful resources. Records for Wingerworth, Chesterfield and Derby can be found at **www.connorsgenealogy.com/Derbyshire**.

A one village genealogical study for Rosliston at **www.rootsweb. ancestry.com/~engcrosl** includes photos of gravestones at St Mary's churchyard, whilst a similar site exists for Smalley at **www.smalley-ops.co.uk/smalleyops.html**. For Cromford village, **www.cromford village.co.uk** contains records for the 1670 hearth tax, a comprehensive time line, and a list of names from the local war memorial, whilst Scarliffe is well served by **www.scarcliffeweb.co.uk**, with census records for 1851–61 and 1891–1901, landowners listed in the poor rate assessment of 1832, and several directories. Other sites to carry useful genealogical records include **www.ashover.org** for Ashover, **http:// freepages.genealogy.rootsweb.ancestry.com/~dlhdby** for Crich, **www. belper-research.com/index.html** for Belper, and **http://webspace. webring.com/people/me/emma4/newhall.html** for Newhall.

Many sites also provide useful parish histories, such as that for Aston at **www.aston-on-trent.co.uk** and Whitewell parish at **www.wlhg.co. uk/index.htm**. Cutthorpe is covered at **www.cutthorpe-derbyshire. co.uk** whilst Matlock and Matlock Bath's histories are recorded at **www.andrewspages.dial.pipex.com/matlock/index.htm**. Heanor and District Local History Society's site at **www.heanorhistory.org.uk** covers the village and surrounding area, whilst a similar site for Ilkeston exists at **www.ilkestonhistory.org.uk**. Baptist Church baptismal and birth records for several parishes in Derbyshire can also be freely sourced at **http://tinyurl.com/yjfbaur**. The Midland Railway Study Centre site at **www.midlandrailway studycentre.org.uk** contains an online catalogue for its holdings on the local rail industry and Billy Riley's Pitwork site on his coal mining memories is well worth visiting at **www.dmm-pitwork.org.uk/html/ index.htm**.

Devonshire

Devon Libraries' Local Studies Service website (**www.devon.gov.uk/ localstudies**) hosts a timeline of the county's history, early maps, a historical gazetteer, online catalogues, a search facility indexing names from various sources held by the archive, and more. The Friends of Devon's Archives site (**www.foda.org.uk**) also carries five major transcription projects, in the form of *Devon and Exeter Oath Rolls 1723*, records from the Episcopal Visitations for 1744 and 1779, lists of Devon freeholders from 1711–99, tithes records from 1838, and a *Black History Project* tracing records on the county's black community as far back as the late sixteenth century. Devon Family History Society and several local records offices are also collaborating on the *Devon Wills Project* at **http://genuki.cs.ncl.ac.uk/DEV/DevonWillsProject**, to act as a finding aid for all surviving copies of pre-1858 wills, many of which were lost in the Second World War.

Several topographical and historical resources for Devon, including a map from 1765 and an entry from Samuel Lewis' 1831 Topographical Dictionary can be found at **www.lerwill-life.org.uk/history/devtales. htm**, whilst nineteenth century tithe maps are at the University of Exeter's Public Participation in Archaeology site (**http://projects.exeter. ac.uk/devonclp/welcome.htm**).

A Florida-based site at **http://turnertree.net** provides a comprehensive list of churches across the whole county, as well as some post office directory descriptions, Devon newspaper extracts from 1913, biographies on famous Devonians, and soldiers buried in the Devonshire Cemetery at the Somme. For Exeter, **www.exetermemories.co.uk** hosts many articles and lists such as *Exeter's Executed* from 1285–1943, a World War 1 Roll of Honour, police photos and more. Exeter City Council's Bereavement Services department has also uploaded alphabetical index cards for over 100,000 burials in the city's three municipal cemeteries at **http://pub.exeter.gov.uk/asp/bereavement**. Torquay is covered by **http://myweb.tiscali.co.uk/terryleaman/index.html**, with many old photos, several directories from 1822–1911, descriptions of places of worship (all denominations), several war memorials and a roll of honour, whilst additional material can be found at **http://content. swgfl.org.uk/seaside/torbay.htm**. For Dartmoor, over 8000 images, as well as articles on the area's history, can be found at **www.dartmoor archive.org**.

An Online Parish Clerks scheme is currently being developed at **http:// genuki.cs.ncl.ac.uk/DEV/OPCproject.html#Listing**, with volunteers providing free look-ups for the parishes for which they hold material, whilst at **http://tinyurl.com/ycmvf7u** the Devon Parishes Index provides links to many online resources.

The village of Chardstock, part of Dorset until its relocation into Devonshire in 1896, is particularly well served with records tran-scriptions by the website of the Chardstock Historical Record Group Web Museum at **www.chardstockwebmuseum.org**, whilst a vast range

The Devonshire-based Chardstock's virtual museum. Courtesy of Chadstock Historical Record Group

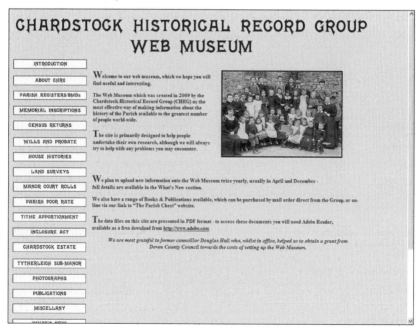

of material for Petrockstowe can be found at **www.petrockstowe.co.uk**. For South Hams, **http://homepages.ihug.co.nz/~our4bears/index.html** provides several parish indexes, monumental inscriptions and 1841 census transcripts.

Moreton History Society's *Virtual Archive* at **www.moretonhampstead. org.uk** has parish records, the religious census from 1851, newspaper cuttings, maps and miscellaneous texts on the parish. Westleigh Parish Council's site (**www.westleigh-devon.gov.uk/history/history_index. htm**) hosts many local resources including a guide to local manors, christenings and marriages from 1561–1697, hearth tax and muster roll records, and more. Sutcombe is also catered for online with an 1845 tithe map, land tax records, trade directory, Domesday book entries and protestation returns from 1642 at **www.sutcomberecords.co.uk**.

A site for Brixham is located at **www.brixhamheritage.org.uk**, with some indexed resources and a maritime archive. A parish site for Luppitt exists at **www.luppitt.net**, including a forum, maps and photographs, and there's a history for South Molton at **www.northdevonlink. co.uk/south-molton.htm**.

Finally, heading offshore, an interactive multimedia Flash movie presentation on the history of Lundy Island can be viewed at **www. lundyisland.co.uk**. For a list of mariners recorded there in the 1881 census visit **www.angelfire.com/de/BobSanders/Lundy81.html**.

Dorset

Dorset has an Online Parish Clerk website at **www.opcdorset.org**, providing extensive coverage for virtually all of the county's parishes, operating in a similar manner to the Cornish equivalent (see p. 64). Equally impressive is the Dorset Parish Registers Index at **www. rootsweb.ancestry.com/~engdorse/PRBT.html** with various databases for parish records from across the county. The Origins Network website carries a respectable database of over 150,000 marriages for the county from 1538–1856, sourced from registers and bishops' transcripts, which includes some nonconformist records. For more information on Dorset-based churches, visit Michael Day's excellent site **http://people.bath. ac.uk/lismd/dorset/churches/**.

The Blackmore Vale site (**www.westcountrygenealogy.com**) carries resources for Gillingham, Oborne, Pulham, Sherborne, Stalkbridge and Sturnminster Newton, such as the 1835 Robson's Directory and bishops' transcripts records. The Dorset Index (**http://freepages.genealogy. rootsweb.ancestry.com/~pbtyc/Dorset.html**) has further records for the Portland area, including monumental inscriptions for Strangers Cemetery and naval and military burials at the Royal Naval Cemetery, as well as a page helpfully showing a list of towns and villages which have moved in and out of the county across time with successive boundary changes.

For Bere Regis you should visit **www.bereregis.org/VillageHistory. htm** to find extensive parish register transcriptions, Domesday Book returns, maps, archaeological notes, and more. Tarrant Crawford is covered at **http://homepages.nildram.co.uk/~jimella/trnscrpt.htm# dorset**, with the site hosting the 1841–1861 and 1881 censuses, and bishops' transcripts.

A timeline for the history of Bournemouth is at **http://content.swgfl. org.uk/seaside/Bmouth.htm**, whilst the South Dorset History Society site (**http://members.multimania.co.uk/SDHS**) has a Weymouth history guide, several historical articles about the area, and bibliographies on military sources and famous people from the area. A timeline and bibliography for Burtoin Bradstock exists at **www.burtonbradstock. org.uk/History/History.htm**, a site which also includes an online photo exhibition, material on the village at war, maps and tithe info, the 1861 census, and more.

On the mapping front, the Dorset Page at **www.thedorsetpage.com** includes Victorian maps, and maps of Dorset hundreds, as well as an additional resource on boundary changes and the Dorset Poll Book from 1807. The Dorset Coast Digital Archive at **www.dcda.org.uk** also hosts Tithe Apportionment maps and the actual digitised apportionment records for the parish of Arne, thought these are at such a poor resolution that they are virtually illegible. The village of Belchalwell has a wonderful site at **www.belchalwell.org.uk** which has many maps for the area, including an 1840 tithe map with records of those eligible to pay tithes.

Durham
The historic county of Durham is well served with online indexes to statutory records, and certificates for most of the county can be ordered through an online system at **www.durham.gov.uk/pages/Service.aspx? ServiceId=663**. Various areas which were once part of the historic county and which have since been established as separate local authorities also have similar services. Records for Gateshead can be searched at **http:// online.gateshead.gov.uk/bmd**, whilst Darlington has a service at **www. darlington.gov.uk/living/register+office/regofficesearch.htm**. For South

Tyneside visit **http://tinyurl.com/23x9z9**, for Sunderland consult **www. sunderland.gov.uk/Index.aspx?articleid=1399**, and for Middlesbrough, Hartlepool, Stockton-on-Tees and Redcar and Cleveland, you should visit **www.teesvalley-indexes.co.uk**.

Over three million pay-per-view records, in the form of baptisms, marriages, burials and census material, are hosted at **www.durham recordsonline.com**, and includes complete coverage for Anglican marriages in the county from 1811–1837. The Joiner Marriage Index at **www.joinermarriageindex.com** carries over 180,000 pre-1837 marriages for Durham, with all but two parishes covered. A look-up exchange also exists at **www.redmire.net/lookup/dur.html** predominantly provides for access to census and monumental inscription through volunteers holding the records.

A history of Sunderland's Mormon community can be found at **www. sunderlandward.co.uk**, along with a cemetery index. The Mormon's FamilySearch Record Search Pilot site at **http://pilot.familysearch.org**

An impressive pay-per-view database resource for Durham-based research. Courtesy of Durham Records Online

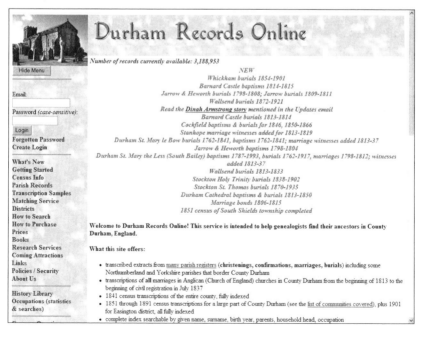

also carries bishops' transcripts for records from the Diocese of Durham from 1700–1900, which includes digitised records for Durham, York and Northumberland. These images can currently only be browsed and not searched by name.

Durham University Library's North East Inheritance Project site at **http://familyrecords.dur.ac.uk/nei/index.htm** is a project that promises a great deal in the near future. It is aiming to create a digital image catalogue of over 150,000 probate records from 1527–1857, covering County Durham, Tyne and Wear and Northumberland. The site already hosts several online exhibitions on various subjects from bankers to the twine maker Thomas Robson, and detailed background information on the history and types of probate records.

The Durham County Records Office online catalogue at **www.durham recordoffice.org.uk/recordoffice/register.nsf/$$searchdcc** includes over 40,000 historic photos from the county which are free to access. Equally useful is the Tomorrow's History site at **www.tomorrows-history.com**, which carries a catalogue and some images for the county, such as a digitised copy of *Bailey's Agriculture of the County of Durham* from 1810, and a great deal of material for Darlington and other towns. An excellent history project for the east of the county is located at **www. east-durham.co.uk**, a site designed to 'capture and preserve photographs, memories of past times and experiences before they are lost and forgotten'.

In addition to the Durham Mining Museum website (see p. 49), the Durham Miner (**www.durham-miner.org.uk**) includes material on everything from local collieries to brass bands, and which also has a handy *Miner Mapping* facility, which hosts maps for villages and towns across the entire county from the nineteenth century to 2004. Further resources for Durham's coal mining district are also located at **www. durhamrecordsonline.com/literature/literature_index.php**, with records including a list of inhabitants in Bishopwearmouth in 1567, hearth tax returns for Monkwearmouth in 1666 and 1674, and an electoral and trade register for Greater Seaham from 1833. A database including entries from Slater's 1854 trade directory of Durham is also available at **http://tinyurl.com/4pyhmr**.

Silksworth Colliery is dealt with at **www.silksworthheritagegroup. org.uk**, along with other aspects of the area's history, whilst a site commemorating the fallen of Silksworth and Tunstall in the First World War is found at **www.tunsilk.co.uk**. For South Hylton, various resources have been made available at **www.shlhs.com**, including some post 1837 parish register material and various trade directories.

Sunderland's maritime heritage is examined at **www.sunderland maritimeheritage.org.uk/index.html**, whilst the history of Hartlepool's shipyards, and the ships built there, is explored at **www.hartlepool built.co.uk**.

Essex

Essex county record offices's online SEAX catalogue at **http://seax. essexcc.gov.uk** has complete details for all of the archive's holdings. It allows you to search for information on records held at the parish level, including details of parish records, electoral registers, poor law records, marriage bonds, vehicle registrations and more.

The History House site at **www.historyhouse.co.uk**, which invites you to 'dip into the history of Essex', is another excellent gateway site with links to resources for each individual town and village in the county, as well as a transcribed version of Daniel Defoe's 1722 work *Tour through the Eastern Counties of England*. For the east of the county you should also visit **www.essex-family-history.co.uk**, which has transcriptions of every possible type of genealogical record you can think of, whilst a sister site at **www.essex-country-life.co.uk** provides resources on farming life in the county and on pastimes.

Essex churches are well recorded photographically if you wish to see where your ancestors worshipped, with two websites of particular interest. The first, located at **www.essexchurches.info**, has images of churches still in existence, whilst the other, at **www22.brinkster.com/ barham/LostChurches.asp**, concerns those no longer standing.

There are no major parish and census records sites covering all of Essex, though the Foxearth and District Local History Society site at **www.foxearth.org.uk** has extracts from various newspapers from 1740–1952, and various north Essex census records and indexes. A wills database for the whole county from 1565–1571 is available at **www. newenglandancestors.org/database_search/ew.asp**, a New England-based family history society site, though you need to be a member to gain access.

An impressive site for the village of Earls Colne at **http://linux02. lib.cam.ac.uk/earlscolne/** hosts material from 1375–1854, including parish registers, censuses, court records, manorial records, and personal records, with gems such as the diary of seventeenth-century vicar

Ralph Josselin. The history of Henham at **www.henhamhistory.org** has parish birth and marriage indexes, as well as wills of parish residents and census indexes, whilst Buckhurst Hill is well catered for at **www.buckhurst-hill-history.btik.com**, with a useful genealogy section including census records, aircraft crew death records and war memorial names. Also on the war memorial front, Chingford's sacrifice in the Great War is commemorated at **www.chingfordwarmemorial.co.uk**, with links on the page to sister sites for Walthamstow, Leytonstone, Forest Gate, Leyton, and Highams Park.

The Camulos site (**www.camulos.com**) covers Colchester, with resources on war memorials listings, local witches, inns, pubs and taverns, King Arthur and more. The names of accused witches and their accomplices from earlier times are also indexed online at **www. hulford.co.uk/towns.html**. An equally varied site is that for Bures Hamlet and Bures St Mary at **www.bures-online.co.uk** which covers the area's history from 1900–2010, with subjects ranging from the women's land army to local dragon myths. Other useful history sites include an excellent photo resource site for Romford at **www.romford. org**, and the deeply impressive Wivenhoe site at **www.wivenhoe. gov.uk/OralHistory/sea_change.htm**, which contains transcribed interviews recorded in the area as part of an oral history project produced for a local history book.

On the law and order front, the history of Essex police, with many past cases explored through an online magazine entitled *History Notebook*, is available at the Essex Police Museum site at **www.essex. police.uk/museum/history.htm**.

Gloucestershire and Bristol
Gloucestershire Archives has a *Genealogical Database* at **ww3.gloucester shire.gov.uk/genealogy/Search.aspx** which allows you to search for wills and administrations from 1541–1858, inventories from 1587–1800, gaol records, overseers' records, and church records.

Monumental inscriptions for several parishes in Gloucestershire, as well as photographs of many churches, can be found at **www. wishful-thinking.org.uk/genuki/GLS/index.html**, whilst additional church images can be further found at **www.allthecotswolds.com**. The GlosGen site (**www.glosgen.co.uk**) has many records of war memorials from across the county, with some additional, though minimal, parish record material. A useful portal site with some further links for the whole county of Gloucestershire can be found at **http://homepages. nildram.co.uk/~jimella/gloucs.htm**.

The Forest of Dean Family History Pages project (**www.forest-of-dean. net**) includes a database of wills as extracted from probate calendars for the west of the county (1858–1941), e-books, village descriptions, parish records, maps and more. You will need to register with the site, but registration is free. Directory records for the Forest of Dean are also accessible at **http://freepages.genealogy.rootsweb.ancestry.com/ ~cbennett**.

A site on Ampney Crucis at **www.ampneycrucis.f9.co.uk** offers limited resources, though does contain photos of gravestones from 1875–1950 where the inscriptions are still legible. Inscriptions from gravestones at Condicote are online at **www.condicote.freeserve.co.uk**, whilst Cromhall is served at **www.cromhall.com/archive/home.php** with war memorial details and a map from 1889. Records for Bitton and surrounding parishes can be located at **www.bittonfamilies.com**, for

The Forest of Dean Family History project. Credit?

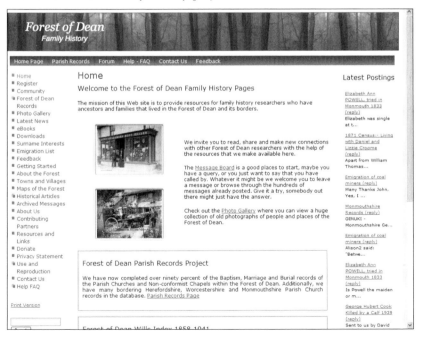

Longhope at **www.longhopevillage.co.uk** and for Taynton at **www. taynton.btinternet.co.uk/index.htm**.

Parish register transcriptions for Ashleworth, Boddington, Bromsberrow, Corse, Deerhurst, Elmstone Hardwicke, Forthampton, Hasfield, Lassington, The Leigh, Norton, Oxenton, Staverton, Tewkesbury, Tirley and Tredington are available at **http://freepages.genealogy.rootsweb. ancestry.com/~wrag44/index.htm**.

The village of Randwick is well served at **www.randwicksources. org.uk** with parish registers, bastardy bonds, settlement records etc, but the links to these from the home page are written in an extremely tiny font, so you may struggle to read them! The Scribes Alcove site (**www.scribes-alcove.co.uk**) has an equally impressive range of material for Berkeley, Hill, Rockhampton, Stone, Oldbury-upon-Severn and Thornbury. The Thornbury Roots site at **www.thornburyroots.co.uk** contains a history of the village street by street, as well as a searchable monumental inscriptions database, voters lists and more, with access gained via the 'Thornbury Sources' button on the home page, whilst additional resources for the area can also be found via **www. mythornbury.co.uk/thornbury/local_history**. For the civil parish of Winterbourne, parish magazines, school records and the usual BMD and census records can be found at **www.frenchaymuseumarchives. co.uk**.

A history of Gloucestershire pubs, including searchable databases for both pubs and breweries in the count is online at **www.gloucestershire camra.org.uk/pubs/glospubs/new**, and if you are up for an extensive pub crawl, a similar site for Bristol is located at **http://bristolslostpubs. eu**, which includes a dedicated discussion forum.

The City of Bristol is sandwiched between Gloucestershire and Somerset. The Bygone Bristol site at **www.gertlushonline.co.uk** has literally hundreds of useful resources, including information on a great many criminal cases and thousands of old photos. Whilst the home page concentrates on images, visit the site map to really see the true potential of the project. An index to wills from 1781–1858, as held by Bristol Records Office, is available at **http://tinyurl.com/ycg25zb**, with earlier coverage to be added in due course.

The local family history society, Bristol and Avon, has some useful resources on its site at **www.bafhs.org.uk**, including the National Burial Index for the area, with the place of abode included (not included on the FindmyPast version), a Bristol Home Children project page and a list of places of worship in the city. Bristol records are included within the Somerset Online Parish Clerks site (**wsom-opc.org.uk**).

Hampshire

A detailed 88 page guide to family history research has been produced by Hampshire Genealogy Society and made available in PDF format at **www.hgs-online.org.uk/hgs_e-books.htm**. Last updated in 2005, it is somewhat out of date in parts, but is still an excellent guide to identifying locally held resources.

Hampshire also has an Online Parish Clerk system, hosted at **www. knightroots.co.uk**, the family history site of Southampton-based Linda and Tony Knight. Similar to other county-based OPC sites, it is accessible via the 'Online Transcriptions' tab on the left of the screen. A look-up exchange is also in operation at **http://members.madasafish.com/ ~dolton/**, with volunteer lookups available for various birth, marriage, death, census and wills records, as well as rental rolls for the Fleming

Hampshire's OPC project, accessible via the Knightroots site. Courtesy of Linda and Tony Knight, Hampshire OPC Co-ordinators

estates in Hampshire and the Isle of Wight. Historic maps for the county dating back to 1575 can be perused via the Old Hampshire Mapped Site at **www.geog.port.ac.uk/webmap/hantsmap/hantsmap**.

More locally, parish records for Botley from 1679–1837 are available at **http://mickcooper.ulmb.com/Mick/bot/bot.htm**, with marriage records handily indexed for both spouses. The village of Froyle's parish records are very comprehensively covered at **www.froyle.com/contents.htm**, with census records included. For Blendworth, Colemore, East Meon, Farringdon, Herriard, Newton Valence and Priors Dean you should visit **http://tinyurl.com/yc84zf7**. If you have connections to Rownhams and North Baddesley then it is well worth visiting **http://homepage. ntlworld.com/sandra.s**, one of the best Hampshire-based genealogy sites around, packed with extracts from directories, parish registers, and other records, including fourteenth century records of The Order of the Knights Hospitallers of St John of Jerusalem.

Further parish records for St. Mary's Crawley (1649–1930), St. Catherine's Littleton (1736–1930) and St Stephen's Sparsholt with Lainston (1609–1930) can be found at the Downs Benefice site at **www.downs-benefice.hampshire.org.uk** (bottom right corner for the relevant links), whilst parish and census records for Dursley are located at **www.durleyvillage.com**. Burials for Blendworth from 1813–1899 can be examined at **http://tinyurl.com/yzxj7pr**, whilst those from the nineteenth and twentieth centuries for St George's Waterlooville are indexed at **www.stgeorgesnews.org/registers/graveyard.htm**, along with baptisms, weddings and burials from 1997–2010.

For the history of Longparish, East Aston, West Aston. Middleton and Forton, visit **www.longparish.org.uk/history/cover.htm** for various resources including subsidy rolls for the area from 1586, the heart tax from 1665, and more. The Hearth Tax for the hundred of Kingsclere is available at **http://tinyurl.com/yk5tfde**, a saved version on the Internet Archive of a site no longer actually up and running. The history of Medstead is well served at **www.medstead.org**, with census records, tithe maps, and a timeline. Alton's past is also explored on the Curtis Museum website at **www3.hants.gov.uk/museum/curtis-museum/ alton-history.htm**.

The south of Hampshire has a long established maritime heritage. The Port Cities website at **www.plimsoll.org/registersAndRecords** contains a comprehensive examination of the history of Southampton, with pages on the Titanic, Southampton at War, various street directories, image galleries, biographies and more. For those with customs connections, **www.customscowes.shalfleet.net** has a history for both Cowes and the Isle of Wight, including newspaper extracts on Cowes from 1800 onwards, record books, lists of customs prosecutions and customs staff.

The Isle of Wight Record Office (**www.iwight.com/library/record_office**) has a copy of *Speed's Atlas* from 1627, as well as various catalogues in the Collections section relating to several of the archive's holdings, such as court records, estate papers, hospitals and work-houses records and more. At the bottom of the page, the archive also has links to pages detailing the extent of its collections of cemeteries records, censuses, electoral registers, manors, monumental inscriptions, newspapers, trade directories and wills. There are databases available for paupers receiving poor relief (1868–1875), and issued alehouse licenses (1766–1819).

The Isle of Wight Family History Society site (**www.isle-of-wight-fhs.co.uk/bmd/startbmd.htm**) has searchable indexes of locally registered births, marriages and deaths from 1837–2002, as well as other data-bases such as monumental inscriptions and burials indexes, census strays, a pedigree index, a photo gallery and a church burials index. Wootton Bridge Historical (**www.woottonbridgeiow.co.uk**) provides information on local history for both Wooton Bridge and the Isle of Wight in general, with over 250 written articles and over a thousand images.

A database of island-based photographers (1840–1940) is online at **www.iowphotos.info**, along with many historical images of local inhabitants. The islands' pubs are explored at **www.insula.vecta.btinternet.co.uk**, whilst a guide to its many memorials and monuments can be found at **www.isle-of-wight-memorials.org.uk**.

Herefordshire
One of the Welsh marches border counties, Herefordshire is not so well served online as its counterparts, but does still have some useful material available.

The Herefordshire Through Time project (**www.herefordshire.gov.uk/htt**) has many wonderful sections devoted to subjects such as work-houses, transport, prisons, agriculture and industry. The Transport section alone includes the history of the county's railways, and the work of the navvies who constructed them. The site also provides access to the county's *Sites and Monuments Records* database, and a *Field*

Names and Landowners database. A map of the marches counties is online at **www.jlb2005.plus.com/wales/tallis/maps/hef.htm**.

Herefordshire Archive Service does not have many resources on its site, though does have a list of registers of property valuations for the Finance Act of 1910 available at **www.herefordshire.gov.uk/leisure/ archives/3584.asp**. The Bromyard History Society at **www.bromyard historysociety.org.uk** outlines the services and resources which the society can provide and also has an online parish map for the district (in the Archive section), as well as some local photos.

Herefordshire Family History Society has some useful material at **www.rootsweb.ancestry.com/~ukhfhs/index.html**, including a monumental inscriptions index for the county, and an index to its journal, *Herefordiensis*. A list of marriages for Bishops Frome from 1754–1799 can be found at **http://tinyurl.com/yk9uj2g**. For the 1830 Pigot's Directory of the county visit **http://tinyurl.com/35ukhwl**; for 1840, **http://tinyurl. com/36psdvm**.

On the military front, the history of the Herefordshire Light Infantry, founded in 1860, is examined at **www.lightinfantry.org.uk/regiments/ hli/hereford_index.htm**.

Hertfordshire

Hertfordshire Archive's site at **www.hertsdirect.org/libsleisure/ heritage1/HALS/indexes** has a useful combined online index to several of its collections which is fully searchable by name. Amongst the collections included are an apprentice index for 1599–1903, fatalities from 1827–1933 (coroners' inquest records), marriages from 1538–1837, newspapers and magazines, parish removals from 1688–1882, and settlements from 1679–1865.

A look-up exchange at **http://graham.rootsweb.ancestry.com/herts_ exchange** allows for access to various types of records across the county, whilst an embryonic gateway site at **www.hertfordshiregenealogy. co.uk** has some useful but limited resources, such as the names of parishes within the counties' various hundreds. The Herts Memories project (**www.hertsmemories.org.uk**) collects old photos and memories from people across the county, and has a useful town and village guide, with links to additional history-based resources.

Paul Joiner's marriage index at **www.joinermarriageindex.co.uk** holds 109,000 marriage records from 133 parishes in Hertfordshire. Paul is also the administrator of the GENUKI page on the county, which can be found on his site at **www.joinermarriageindex.com/pjoiner/**

genuki/ HRT. If you are interested in finding where a marriage took place, photographs of various churches from across the county can be found at **www.iananddot.org/chphoto/hertschurches.htm**.

Parish records for Therfield, along with directories and censuses, are located at **www.therfield.net**, including annual census lists from 1803–1807 and 1821, in addition to the main decennial censuses from 1841 onwards. The site also hosts the wonderful *Parochial Pedigrees* work compiled by the Reverend John Godwin Hale, rector of the parish from 1870–1907. For the village of Redbourne, Chelsea Pensioner names from the 1851 census and militia names from 1758–1786 are amongst the records which can be consulted at **www.redbourn.org.uk/Redbourn/ RedbournGenealogy**. Pirton's local history group site at **www.pirton history.org.uk/Default.aspx** hosts a 'searchable relational database' which can be used to find parish and census records, as well as directories, militia lists, wills and monumental inscriptions. Photos and maps are also available.

Monumental inscriptions for Knebworth Cemetery, burial grounds at Almonds Lane and Weston Road in Stevenage, St Mary's Church in Shephall, Stevenage, and further grounds at Welwyn, Woolmer Green and Hitchin can be accessed at **http://homepage.ntlworld.com/ jeffery.knaggs/MIs.html**. Additional inscriptions for St James the Great, Thorley, along with various parish register transcriptions, can be found at **www.friends.stjames.btinternet.co.uk/index.htm**, whilst inscriptions for Three Close Lane graveyard in Berkhamsted can be viewed at **http://tinyurl.com/yzdx69z**.

Recollections of Rushden, with a pictorial history guide, and timeline of village history, are available at **http://alephzero.tripod.com**, whilst Bishop's Storford enjoys a series of history guides to the area at **www. stortfordhistory.co.uk**, covering everything from individual streets to the local leather industry. The Bovingdon village website at **www. bovingdon.org** includes local history notes, photos and Bovingdon School log book extracts from 1890–1927, whilst a history of Barkley, with a map and some aerial photos, is available at **www.barley-village. co.uk/the_village.htm**.

If there were genealogical website awards given out, one site definitely worthy of nomination is Barbara Chapman's splendid effort, the *Leverstock Green Chronicle*, located at **http://lgchronicle20.homestead. com/index.html**. A detailed labour of love, the project hosts practically every sort of historical record and essay under the sun.

Huntingdonshire

The historic county of Huntingdonshire now forms the western part of modern Cambridgeshire. Confusingly, the north of the old county, containing Peterborough, was briefly part of Northamptonshire also. As such, many records for Huntingdonshire can also be found within both Cambridgeshire and Northamptonshire repositories. Cambridgeshire Archives' catalogue (**www.cambridgeshire.gov.uk/leisure/archives/catalogue**) contains details of all of Huntingdonshire's old parish records and additional resources, whilst the CAMDEX system (see p. 60) also carries modern statutory records indexes for Huntingdonshire.

A county look-up exchange exists at **http://aztecrose.tripod.com/huntingdon/hun.html**, whilst Huntingdonshire Family History Society's website (**www.huntsfhs.org.uk/MembersPages.html**) has a link to various members' pages, such as Martyn Smith's interesting history of Huntingdonshire cyclist battalions at **www.huntscycles.co.uk**. Cambridgeshire FHS's Boer War deaths database at **www.cfhs.org.uk/BoerWarDeaths** also covers Huntingdonshire. For records from Fenstanton, visit **www.fenstanton-village.co.uk**. The history of Somersham is dealt with at **www.somersham.info**.

A list of mayors of Huntingdon from 1800–1840 exists at GENUKI, but a further list of mayors for the whole county in 1902 is also listed at **www.rootsweb.ancestry.com/~enghun**, with the site also carrying additional resources such as a section on Huntingdon railways and a gazetteer.

Finally, the history of Huntingdonshire Methodism is explored at **www.rootsweb.ancestry.com/~engcam/method.htm**.

Kent

An online parish clerk site for Kent is slowly building momentum at **www.kent-opc.org**, whilst a volunteer-based look-up exchange is also in operation at **http://jo42.tripod.com/knt.html**. The *Kent Genealogy* site at **http://freepages.genealogy.rootsweb.ancestry.com/~mrawson** also carries a significant amount of material, including parish register transcriptions, quarter session records, probate records and census and directory entries. A detailed parish gazetteer of West Kent is available via **www.nwkfhs.org.uk**, where you will also find free census and monumental inscriptions databases.

Medway Council's archive service has an online database of holdings available through its *CityArk* site at **http://cityark.medway.gov.uk** and includes a significant collection of digitised parish registers which can be browsed, and a marriage index for the years 1837–1911. Various other collections are also present, including shipping registers, licensing records and burial records for a limited number of parishes.

The *Research Section* of the Kent Archaeological Society website at **www.kentarchaeology.org.uk** includes a substantial number of monumental inscriptions from across the county, exchequer pipe rolls, 6 inch scale OS maps from 1905/08, wills transcriptions and more. Various essays on the county's history can also be accessed at **www.heres historykent.org.uk/index.cfm**, along with an impressive timeline.

A comprehensive collection of records for Folkestone is available at **http://freepages.genealogy.rootsweb.ancestry.com/~folkestonefamilies** though when you first access the homepage you would be as well to turn off your computer's speakers, as what can only be described as a disconcerting blast of noise hits you – various pages on the site are further blessed with bells peeling and all sorts to slowly drive you mad! The resources themselves are limited, though there are some interesting essays and some excellent census material. Bishops transcripts for Farnborough from 1813–1850 are at **http://tinyurl.com/2u9de2g**, whilst a marriage index for parishes in the mid-Kent area from 1754–1911 can be found at **http://woodchurchancestry.org.uk/midkentmarriages**. A Dover 'scrapbook' at **http://doversociety.homestead.com/DoverHistory Scrapbook.html** is quite literally that, with a real mixture of anecdotes, resources and images, whilst the history of Dover's hostelries is recorded at **www.dover-kent.com**.

The parish of Northbourne is well provided for at **http://freespace. virgin.net/andrew.parkinson4** with tithe records, poll books, directories, memorial listings and more, whilst the Isle of Sheppey is equally well served at **http://freepages.genealogy.rootsweb.ancestry.com/~penney**. Resources for Staplehurst are at **http://tinyurl.com/yak62lb**, including probate indexes, censuses, parish registers, tithe awards and monumental inscriptions, whilst the Kemsing Heritage Centre site (**www. kemsingheritagecentre.org.uk**) has some interesting material, such as a list of patients and staff working at the local VAD hospital in the First World War.

Various projects are available for Sittingbourne. The local museum site (**www.sittingbourne-museum.co.uk**) provides a general background to the area, as well as a series of monumental inscriptions at **http:// tinyurl.com/ygfytc7** for Borden Churchyard. The *Sittingbourne Remembers* site (**www.pigstrough.co.uk/ww1/index.html**) has a great deal of historic content commemorating the stories of local Sittingbourne and Milton

Regis soldiers who fought in the First World War. Additional war memorial projects for the county include the Kent Fallen site (**www. kentfallen.com**), Faded Genes (**www.fadedgenes.co.uk**) and the Dover War Memorial project (**www.doverwarmemorialproject.org.uk**).

Over 2000 photographs from Maidstone Museum on aspects of Kent history are online at **www.kentphotoarchive.org.uk**, whilst images of churches from across the county can be viewed at **www.kentchurches. info**, with some accompanying contextual information for each. Additional church images can also be found at **www.roughwood.net/ ChurchAlbum/ChurchFrames.htm**, whilst various old photos and postcards of East Kent towns and villages are online at **www.eastkent. freeuk.com**.

An image of Canterbury Cathedral taken from a magic lantern projection slide, one of many images available online from Kent photo Archive. Courtesy of kentphotoarchive.org.uk

Lancashire

The historic County Palatine of Lancashire was the heart of the industrial north, taking in many cities such as Manchester, Liverpool and Lancaster, as well as several towns and villages. A digitised copy of the 1854 publication *The Pictorial History of the County of Lancaster* provides a useful overview of the county's history at **www.archive.org/ details/pictorialhistor00unkngoog**.

A useful gateway site for Lancashire resources is online at **www. aboutlancs.com**, whilst an online parish clerk site is available at **www.lan-opc.org.uk**. The latter includes a county map and parish list, with the clerk for each parish contactable by e-mail via a link on the left hand side of each parish page. Indexes for locally held statutory indexes for the county are available at **www.lancashirebmd.org.uk**.

Lancashire's record office has a useful set of downloadable guides at **www.lancashire.gov.uk/education/record_office** which lists its holdings for Church of England, nonconformist and Roman Catholic parish records. There is also an online database of county police records from 1840–1925, which includes some borough force records for Rochdale, Southport, Preston and Wigan, and an online catalogue for the whole archive entitled LANCAT. Another handy council site is Lancashire Lantern (**www.lantern.lancashire.gov.uk**), which carries e-resources on a variety of themes, such as an image archive, a pioneers section, and a library catalogue.

The county's cotton weaving industry is explored at **www.spinning theweb.org.uk**, and includes maps, photos, and place descriptions. Also worth exploring is **www.cottontimes.co.uk**, and **www.cottontown.org**, which goes into particular depth on Blackburn and Darwen.

The Pastfinder site (**www.gmcro.co.uk/gmpf/index.htm**) has a catalogue of over four thousand collections held within the Greater Manchester area, whilst Manchester and Lancashire Family History Society has a guide on the city's cemeteries at **www.mlfhs.org.uk/Infobase/index.htm**. The city's archive has an online catalogue hosted at **www.manchester. gov.uk/libraries/arls**, which also contains a list of its parish record holdings, whilst the Manchester UK site (**www.manchester2002-uk. com**) has gazetteers and historical maps of Greater Manchester and Lancashire. Various additional guides and resources can be found at **www.manchester-family-history-research.co.uk**, a site which is particularly useful for researching local prisons in the area amongst other subjects. A searchable database of publicly contributed memories and resources for Trafford may also be of use at **www.trafford.gov.uk/ content/tca**.

Due to water damage in several 1851 census returns for Greater Manchester following a flood, a great deal of information was rescued using sophisticated retrieval techniques by TNA and Manchester and Lancashire FHS. This has since been made available at FindmyPast, but free surname and street indexes for the records for Manchester, Chorlton-on-Medlock, Salford, Ashton-under-Lyme and Oldham are available at **www.1851-unfilmed.org.uk**.

On the Mersey, the *Port Cities* Liverpool page at **www.portcities. org.uk** has essays on slavery, the Blitz and more. *Liverpool History Projects* at **www.liverpoolhistoryprojects.co.uk** carries a great deal of Roman Catholic records for the city, a First World War database of Liverpool's Fallen Heroes, information on the Liverpool Irish Regiments, a list of Merseyside immigrants applying for naturalisation from 1879–1912, and the *Death in the Pool of Life* site, with details on the locations of burial and death records. An online database for nineteenth century baptisms, marriages, burials and pauper burials at St Anthony's Liverpool is also found at **http://stanthonys-liverpool.com/project/index.php**. For a virtual tour of the city in 1825 visit **http://liverpool-1825.tripod.com**, whilst further material on the city's hinterland can also be examined at **www.roydenhistory.co.uk**. On the newspaper front, **http://jeffmax. pwp.blueyonder.co.uk/abe_max.html** carries articles from the *Liverpool Jewish Gazette* from 1968–1970, whilst additional newspaper extracts can be found at **www.old-merseytimes.co.uk** and **www.old-liverpool. co.uk**. A list of prisoners and staff from Walton Gaol in 1881 is at **www. rootsweb.ancestry.com/~engchs/WAL.html**.

Rochdale's **www.link4life.org** site includes essays on topics such as child labour, coal mining and engineering, as well as several history-based e-books and a local studies catalogue. The material is accessed through the Arts and Heritage section, then by visiting the Local Studies link. For Oldham, useful research guides are available at **http://tinyurl.com/yvdsdr**, whilst an online searchable image guide for Ashton-under-Lyme is located at **www.tameside.gov.uk/localstudies**. A catalogue for Bury Archives is also available at **http://archives.bury. gov.uk**.

Workhouse records for 1871 for Lancaster, Walsden and Preston are to be found at **http://tinyurl.com/yzv57c7**, and a Lancaster convict database for the early nineteenth century at **www.lancastercastle.com/ home.php**. Resources for Bolton at **http://tinyurl.com/ybkbbyq** include lists of special constables from 1816–1831, workhouse birth registers, marriage licenses, and more. Cemetery records for Wigan can be consulted at **www.wiganworld.co.uk/stuff**.

There are many other excellent sites for smaller settlements around the county. Parish records and other resources for Todmorden and Walsden are available at **http://todmordenandwalsden.co.uk**, whilst the villages cleared to make way for the Stocks Reservoir in the Dalehead Valley are commemorated at **www.dalehead.org**. Materials for Cronton, Halewood, Huyton, Kirkby, Knowsley village, Prescot, Roby, Tarbock and Whiston can be found at the Knowsley Local History site at **http://history.knowsley.gov.uk**. For the 1841 and 1871 census for Hurst and surrounding districts, visit **www.c5d.co.uk/homepage.htm**.

Finally, for a dose of a world gone mad, explore the stories of the Pendle Witches at the brilliant **www.pendlewitches.co.uk**.

Leicestershire
There is a Leicestershire online parish clerk site at **www.rootsweb. ancestry.com/~engleiopc**, but many links on the parish pages were found not to be working at the time of writing, the site not having been updated for over a year and a half. However, there are some useful resources still available, including maps, photos and census records. A Leicestershire people index is also available at **http://members. multimania.co.uk/larpindex/home.php**, with names of soldiers, convicts and paupers as extracted from sources at TNA and local archives.

A guide for holdings at Leicestershire's records office is available at **http://tinyurl.com/ykzfyk6**, whilst a gateway site for information on the county's many villages is online at **www.leicestershirevillages. com**, containing links to several locally-based history projects.

For images and details of churches across the county, visit **www. leicestershirechurches.co.uk**. The Leicestershire and Rutland Family History Society also provides free church images from the county at it site at **www.lrfhs.org.uk**, and offers a free e-mail look-up service for Methodist register entries from across the county. Baptist records for several parishes, including some monumental inscriptions, can also be freely sourced at **http://tinyurl.com/yjfbaur**.

Many records for Leicestershire are found on Guy Etchells' website at **http://freespace.virgin.net/guy.etchells**, including parish register transcriptions for Muston, Bottesford, Eastwell, Quorndon, Long Clawson, Wartnaby and Hoton, as well as maps, wills and more. Village resources for Redmile, in the county's north east, including marriages, censuses and directories, can be found at **www.redmilearchive.freeuk.com**, whilst Ratcliffe Culey, Sheepy Magna, Sibson, Orton-on-the-Hill, and Twycross are all catered for at **www.mdlp.co.uk/resources/lei.htm**, with monumental inscriptions, marriage and poor law records, history notes and picture galleries. Tilton on the Hill is also dealt with at **www. tiltononthehill.org.uk**, but the writing is very faint and hard to read. Bear with it though, as it has a useful parish record database and census transcriptions for the village.

Coalville's history is explored at **www.coalville-heritage.info/home. html**, and includes an interesting pronunciation guide for phrases in the local dialect, whilst Whitwick's past is recorded at **www.whitwick. org.uk/opener.php**. The history of the local tanning and mining industries surrounding Swannington can be read at **www.swannington-heritage. co.uk**.

Lincolnshire
There are several county wide resources for Lincolnshire. A convict transportation database exists at the county archives site at **http:// tinyurl.com/yjzsgbk**, along with an index to consistory court wills and lists of parish registers and bishops transcripts held at the facility. The Cultural Collections website at **http://tinyurl.com/yhob6d9** provides a wider database search facility for over half a million items in various other county-based archives, libraries and museums, whilst lay sub-sidy rolls for various settlements across the county are hosted by the University of Leicester at **www.le.ac.uk/english/pot/lincers.html**.

A marriage index from 1837–1870 for sixteen Lincolnshire registration districts is found at **http://s10.freefronthost.com/mi**, whilst volunteer-based look-up exchanges exist at both **http://williamsgwynfa.tripod. com** and **www.genealogy-links.co.uk/html/lin.lookup.html**. On the military front, a county wide war memorial project is online at **www. memorial-lincs.org.uk**. For newspapers, Lincolnshire's family history society (**www.lincolnshirefhs.org.uk**) hosts extracts from various editions from 1780–1929, and provides a handy parish map.

The Wisbech and the Fenlands site (**http://contueor.com/wisbech**) hosts records for Lincolnshire, Cambridgeshire and Norfolk, with a searchable database of almost eighteen thousand records. Transcriptions of post 1813 baptismal and marriage registers for several parishes are at **http://wparkinson.com/transcriptions.htm**, whilst the site's creator Wendy Parkinson has also uploaded over 1200 church photos from the county at **www.wparkinson.com/Churches/Guide.htm**, taken by both her and Paul Fenwick. The latter has an additional photographs site at **www.imagesoflincolnshire.co.uk**. Photos of gravestones from many churches in the north and north east of the county can be found at **www.rootsweb.ancestry.com/~engggfhg**.

Parish records for Frodingham from 1750 to the early 1800s are available at **www.genogold.com/html/lincolnshire.html**. For Springthorpe, school records, lay subsidy rolls and more can be located at **www. springthorpe-village.org.uk/history**, whilst Sedgebrook is similarly served at **http://myweb.tiscali.co.uk/hampson**, with transcripts of the 1841–1911 censuses, directories, school records, strays and school records. The Metheringham Area Community Leisure Association has an impressive site at **www.macla.co.uk** containing material for Metheringham, Blankney, Dunston, Nocton, Scopwick and Tanvats, including trade directory extracts and the 1881 census.

Finally, for proof that God may in fact be from Lincolnshire, and seriously interested in genealogy, you should visit the fantastic *Axholme Ancestry* site at **www.red1st.com**. Centred on the Isle of Axholme, but also covering a wider area in both Lincolnshire and Yorkshire, the sheer range of digitised resources, databases, manorial rolls, monumental inscriptions and pedigrees is seriously impressive.

London (Greater London including Middlesex)
The former historic county of Middlesex, the second smallest in England, is now in its entirety a part of the Greater London area (which also takes in parts of Essex, Kent, Surrey and Hertforshire). A list of Middlesex parishes is located at **www.angelfire.com/fl/Sumter/ Middlesex.html**, with an additional list and parish maps available at **www.west-middlesex-fhs.org.uk/content/research.aspx**.

It should come as no surprise that the major genealogy vendor sites have provided a great deal of resources online concerning the nation's capital. Ancestry reigns supreme on this front, with its partnership agreement with the London Metropolitan Archives and Guildhall Library Manuscripts to digitise and release records under the banner of the *London Historical Records Collection*, with its own dedicated site at **http://landing.ancestry.co.uk/lma**. This includes birth, marriage and burial registers from 1538–1812, births and baptisms from 1813–1906, marriage registers from 1754–1921, burials from 1813–1980 and Board of Guardians records for the capital's workhouses.

The Origins Network also has several major London centred collections online, including Boyd's Marriage Index from 1538–1840, St. Andrew

The London Historical Records Collection hosted on Ancestry.co.uk Courtesy of Ancestry.co.uk

Holborn Marriage Index 1754–1812, Marriage License Allegations 1694–1850, Archdeaconry Court of London Wills Index 1700–1807, Surrey and South London wills extracts 1470–1856, London Apprenticeship extracts 1442–1850, a London Burials Index for 1538–1853 and a London Consistory Court Depositions Index for 1700–1713. The collections can be independently accessed via **www.londonorigins.com**.

The AIM25 site at **www.aim25.ac.uk** has a searchable catalogue of over a hundred archives, livery companies, societies and more within the M25 area, whilst a catalogue for all of London's libraries can be found at **http://tinyurl.com/yd63txl**. An online catalogue for London Metropolitan Archives is available at **http://tinyurl.com/yd6c2rc**, and its *London Generations* database can be accessed at **www.cityoflondon. gov.uk/londonGenerations**. This includes an index of 23,500 marriage bonds from 1673–1850 for the Diocese of Winchester, for which it is possible to obtain copies of the originals. Over 10,000 Archdeaconry Court of Middlesex Wills from 1609–1810, covering Westminster and

Middlesex, can also be searched at **www.cityoflondon.gov.uk/wills** and copies purchased at £4 each.

The City of Westminster Archive's WESTCAT catalogue (**http://tinyurl. com/yedsqov**) provides some useful indexes such as *St.Martin-in-the-Fields Settlement Examinations* from 1732–1755, a *Survey of London* index to street names, and the *Motco Project*, a database of prints, maps and images of London.

The Institute of Historical Research's Guildhall Library Manuscripts site at **www.history.ac.uk/gh** links to various guides and indexes for business records, livery companies, Lloyd's captains registers, probate inventories from the Peculiar Court of St. Paul's Cathedral and marriage licenses from St. Katharine-by-the-Tower (1686–1802). The London Metropolitan University's Women's Library website, with a catalogue of holdings, is at **www.londonmet.ac.uk/thewomenslibrary**.

Historical paintings and images of the city, and several virtual exhibitions depicting life in London across time, are available at **http:// collage.cityoflondon.gov.uk**. Images from the Illustrated London News Picture Library can also be consulted at **www.iln.org.uk**.

On the cartographic front, the London School of Economics has created a site dedicated to Charles Booth's nineteenth century poverty maps for the city at **http://booth.lse.ac.uk**, with various notebooks and additional resources included. Various nineteenth century cholera maps of the city drawn up by John Snow can also be found at **www.ph.ucla. edu/epi/snow.html**. The **www.oldlondonmaps.com** site does what it says on the tin, and Greenwood's London map of 1827 is available at **http://users.bathspa.ac.uk/greenwood**. A Victorian London A-Z is on-line at **http://homepage.ntlworld.com/hitch/gendocs/lon-str.html**, and an aerial survey of the city taken in 1949 can be viewed at **www. oldaerialphotos.com**.

The London Burials site (**www.londonburials.co.uk**) provides an excellent guide to cemetery locations within Greater London, but does not provide any monumental inscriptions; a similar guide for the east of the city is provided by the area's local family history society at **www.eolfhs.org.uk**, a site which also carries a discussion forum and a detailed parish information guide. The pay-per-view Deceased Online site (**www.deceasedonline.com**) has digitised burial record images from several London boroughs available.

Lee Jackson's *Dictionary of Victorian London* at **www.victorianlondon. org** provides a detailed guide to life in the capital in the late nineteenth century. The Port Cities page at **www.portcities.org.uk/london** has a wider reach examining the city's role from pre-Tudor times to the twentieth century, with resources including a look at the various trades worked at from 1850–1980 and the impact of the Blitz on the Docklands area. A study on the role of bargemen on the Thames is also available at **www.bargemen.co.uk**.

Essays on Tower Hamlets' history are available at **www.mernick.org. uk/thhol**, with indexes for locally recorded statutory birth, marriage and death certificates available at **www.thbmd.co.uk**. The history of the Isle of Dogs is explored at **www.islandhistory.org.uk**. If you have an interest in Tottenham High Road, visit **www.mickbruff.pwp. blueyonder.co.uk/highroad**, which includes resources such as census returns, directory extracts and monumental inscriptions for All Hallows Church. For a similar site on Brentford High Street in Hounslow, visit **www.bhsproject.co.uk**.

The development of areas such as Barnet, Ealing, Greenwich and Kingston, in relation to the city's transport infrastructure, is dealt with by the London Transport Museum at **www.ltmuseum.co.uk/collections/**

A handy guide to life in Victorian London. Courtesy of www.victorianlondon.org

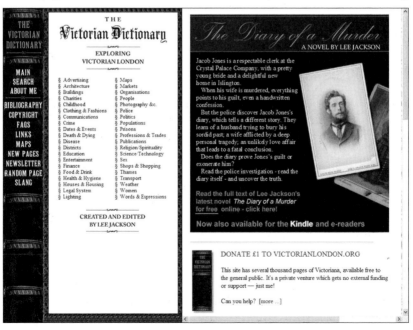

24.aspx, which also provides a guide to the history of Caribbean recruit-ment in the transport services. A Roll of Honour for staff of the London Passenger Transport Board who fell in the Second World War is avail-able at **www.eastkent.freeuk.com/misc/lt_deaths_ww2.htm**, whilst the London and North Western Railway Society has an archive catalogue, a staff history research guide and a further roll of honour at **www. lnwrs.org.uk**.

Other notable industry sites include a database of 9,000 photo-graphers and associated trades folk from 1841–1901 at **www.photo london.org.uk**, a guide to historic Greater London pubs at **http://london publichouse.com**, and a database of entertainers who performed in London's music halls at **www.rhul.ac.uk/drama/Music-hall/index.asp**. Indexes to University of London student graduations from 1836–1926 and examinations registers 1838–1889 are located at **www.shl.lon.ac. uk/apecialcollections/archives/atudentrecords.shtml**.

The Old Bailey site (**www.oldbaileyonline.org**) carries the proceed-ings of almost 200,000 trials from 1674–1913, plus background history resources on crime and enforcement. The history of the Metropolitan Police, with a timeline, books of remembrance and details on its archives can be explored at **www.met.police.uk/history**, whilst a general history of policing in London is at **www.historybytheyard.co.uk**, including gallantry awards list for the twentieth and twenty-first centuries. For Metropolitan Women Police Association story visit **www.metwpa.org. uk/viewpage.php?page_id=1**.

On the medical front, the Historic Hospital Admission Records project at **http://hharp.org** carries resources relating to the early years of three children's hospitals, namely the Hospital for Sick Children at Great Ormond Street, the Evelina Hospital and the Alexandra Hospital for Children with Hip Disease, with over 100,000 individual admission records from 1852 to 1914. For a series of articles on ragged schools in the capital, visit **www.raggedschoolmuseum.org.uk**.

Finally for the capital, if your ancestors were members of the true nobility of London, a list of Pearly Kings and Queens can be found at **www.pearlysociety.co.uk**.

Norfolk
Norfolk County Council's *Norfolk Online Access to Heritage* platform (**www.noah.norfolk.gov.uk**) allows you to view information and digitised resources from several sources in the county, including the

Library Service, the Norfolk Record Office and Norfolk Museums and Archaeology Service. Amongst the holdings are local archive catalogues, newspaper indexes, tithe maps, directories and more – for a full listing use the site's 'Advanced Search' function.

Norfolk Family History Society has a detailed parish guide for the county at **www.norfolkfhs.org.uk** with links to many online resources (mainly at GENUKI), and very usefully names contiguous parishes for each entry. A Norfolk Baptism Project exists at **http://tinyurl.com/nnf4d9**, providing records from 1813–1880, whilst the Norfolk Transcription Archive at **www.genealogy.doun.org/transcriptions/index.php** has parish register transcriptions, subsidy taxes, muster rolls and census returns. Paddy Apling's excellent site at **http://apling.freeservers.com** has directory information, the 1891 census and many more resources for each of the hundreds within the county, broken down to both parish and village level.

Various newspaper entries from the *Norfolk Chronicle* and other rags can be found at **www.foxearth.org.uk/newspapers.html**. On the photographic front, the Norfolk Broads are well covered at **http://people. netcom.co.uk/j.stringe**, and images of churches from across the county can be viewed at **www.norfolkchurches.co.uk**.

The Norfolk Heritage Explorations site (**www.norfolkheritage.org. uk**) covers the history of Mulbarton, Harleston, Happisburgh, Breckles and Reepham, all deliberately chosen as a representative sample of the diverse communities found within the county. The site contains few historic records as such, but carries many recorded memories and images.

A history of Buxton is provided at **www.buxton-norfolk.co.uk/ interest.htm**, whilst the settlement of Mattishall is discussed at **www. mattishall-village.co.uk**. Transcriptions of wills, censuses, enclosure maps, directories, and archdeacons' transcripts for Itteringham, and a useful photographic graveyard survey, are available at **www.itteringham. com/history/history.html**. Serving Deopham is **www.deophamhistory. co.uk**, with transcriptions of the 1911 census, directories, gravestones, maps and tithe records for the area. Census material for Brumstead can be found at **http://tinyurl.com/yawa3o9**, and a local history of Merton can be found at **www.merton.ukgo.com**, including information on the two wars and the village's war memorials.

The interesting **www.salthousehistory.co.uk** site provides some useful material for Salthouse such as maps and poor prisoners returns from 1815, but also recalls the extraordinary story of a parish register dating back to 1538 which had been buried by a rector in World War Two and only recently discovered still buried in the ground.

Other useful resources for the county include a list of gamekeepers from Kelly's Directory 1883 at **http://apling.freeservers.com/Jobs/ Gamekeepers.htm**, a database of Norfolk pubs at **www.norfolkpubs. co.uk**, and the wonderful Norfolk Mills site at **www.norfolkmills.co. uk**, which hosts a list of millers' wills from the seventeenth and eighteenth centuries, names of millers and databases on various types and locations of mills.

Northamptonshire
One of the best Northamptonshire websites is Graham Ward's *Genealogy and Nonconformist History* project at **www.edintone.com**, which is packed with resources on the history of the non-established churches in the county, including a virtual library of books on the subject. If your ancestor was a clock or watchmaker, you are also in luck, as Graham also provides a useful list of those working in the professions, drawn from several sources. Equally fascinating is the Northamptonshire Black History project at **www.northants-black-history.org.uk**, which includes a brilliant searchable database drawn from newspaper extracts, archive holdings and oral history project material.

If your ancestor was a soldier you should visit **www.northants1841. fsnet.co.uk** to explore the Northampton Independent Soldier Photo-graph Index. This contains over three thousand entries from local news-papers written between 1914–1920, eighteenth century militia indexes and a Northampton First World War roll of honour. The site also hosts a wills index from 1854–1857, parish removal indexes, strays, Quaker baptisms and marriages, and travellers recorded in baptismal registers from 1751–1812.

It is every genealogist's dream to travel back in time, and at **www. northants.police.uk/museum_new** you can do just that by stepping into a Police Box at the county police force's online virtual museum, which includes biographies of all the chief constables to have worked at both county and borough level, as well as details of many old cases and murders.

There are no major county wide record transcription projects, but baptisms in Oundle from 1813–1838 can be found at **http://tinyurl. com/ yzbxkw7**, whilst parish and statutory records for Pottersbury can be found at **www.potterspury.org.uk**. The Towcester and District Local Historical Society website at **www.mkheritage.co.uk/tdlhs** also carries several parish register and wills entries. Rushden and surrounding district are catered for at **www.rushdenheritage.co.uk**, with lots of resources on land records, the shoemaking industry, local war memorials, church history and more.

Censuses for Glapthorn can be found at **www.eyemead.com/ glapthor.htm**, and for Burton Latimer at **www.burtonlatimer.info**, whilst directories for Cottingham can be accessed at **www.cottingham history.co.uk**. The history of Duston is recalled at **www.duston.org.uk**, with a roll of honour and memorial inscriptions included, and Helmdon is dealt with at **www.helmdon.com**, with a list of obituaries, monumental inscriptions, picture galleries and press cuttings. For Kettering war memorial information, visit **http://maskew.users.btopenworld. com**.

Northumberland

The *Northumberland Communities* site (**http://tinyurl.com/yfs3671**) provides a detailed history for each village and town in the county, accompanied by photos, digitised manuscripts, ordnance survey maps and census information, making it an essential first port of call. Tyne Lives (**www.tynelives.org.uk**) provides a similar gateway, with oral histories and essays on various subjects such as the fishing industry, the Tynemouth Volunteer Life Brigade, coal mining, and more, whilst Tomorrow's History (**www.tomorrows-history.com**) hosts several Northumberland community history projects.

Newcastle Register Office has placed some limited indexes online at **www.newcastle.gov.uk/core.nsf/a/dfcdeathshistorical#perfsearch** for statutory births (1837–1870) and marriages (1837–1900), which can be used to order up copies of the records. For death, extracts from the *Newcastle Evening Chronicle* have been made available at **www.genuki. org.uk/big/eng/NBL/DeathNotices** for deaths from 1885–1906, indexed by surname. Northumberland and Durham Family History Society has a list of its records holdings for Northumberland at **www.ndfhs.org. uk/Resources_NBL.pdf**, whilst the county records office, now known as Northumberland Collections Service, has an online catalogue at **www3.northumberland.gov.uk/catalogue**. A Northumberland lookup exchange exists at **www.redmire.net/lookup/nbl.html** for various sets of records from across the county.

One of the most exciting projects currently in development is Durham University Library's *North East Inheritance* project at **http:// familyrecords.dur.ac.uk/nei/index.htm**. Though not yet fully up and running at the time of writing, it promises to make available probate records from 1527–1857 via an online digital image catalogue of over 150,000 wills and related archive material from across Northumberland, Durham and Tyne and Wear.

Steve Bulman's site at **www.stevebulman.f9.co.uk/northumberland** reproduces William Whellan and Co.'s *History of Northumberland* gazetteer from 1855. For Gateshead, a useful site with various old maps, postcards, church images and more is located at **www.picturesofgateshead.co.uk/ index.html**.

The Tyneside Family History site (**http://tinyurl.com/yh9fukl**) provides a nineteenth century history of Newcastle and various colliery villages such as Seghill, Cramlington, Killingworth, Burradon, Seaton Burn and Weetslade, with various topics covered including migration, the impact of the Irish, housing, education and work. The Durham Mining Museum project (see p. 49) also contains resources for Northumbrian miners and their communities.

The North East Inheritance project, an important resource for northern probate records. Reproduced by permission of Durham University Library

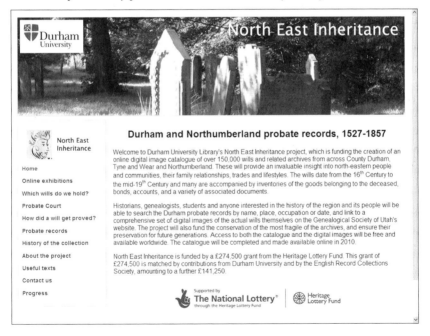

Finally, the Mormons' FamilySearch Record Search Pilot site at **http:// pilot.familysearch.org** carries bishops' transcripts for records from the Diocese of Durham covering the period from 1700–1900. Records for Northumberland are included, though the images can only be browsed and not searched by name.

Nottinghamshire
A catalogue of holdings for Nottinghamshire Archives is available at **http://nawcat.nottinghamshire.gov.uk** whilst Nottinghamshire Local Studies Library hosts an equivalent at **www.nottinghamcity.gov.uk/ libraries**. The county council website also has some interesting online exhibitions at **www.nottinghamshire.gov.uk/home/leisure/archives/ exhibitions.htm** focussing on subjects as diverse as Broad Marsh and Narrow Marsh, the Story of Raleigh Cycles, and Nottingham's Afro-Caribbean heritage. The county's black history is further explored at the Thoroton Society of Nottinghamshire's heritage gateway site at **www. nottsheritagegateway.org.uk**, as well as various other historic topics. The Thoroton Society also has a useful bibliography of county-based literature available at **http://tinyurl.com/yj7ozum**.

An illustrated database of Nottinghamshire churches can be explored at Heather Faulkes' *Old Nottinghamshire* site (**www.oldnotts.co.uk**), as well as the history of the Ashfield, Bidsworth and Mansfield areas. Gazetteer descriptions for several parishes in the county from 1855 can be found at **www.stevebulman.f9.co.uk/northumberland/index.html**, whilst a variety of gazetteers and other resources can be found at **www. charliespage.co.uk/pollbookindex.htm**, including Hodson's Directory from 1814, a 1754 Poll Book for Nottinghamshire and the names of Sherwood Foresters in the Boer War. Various additional resources can also be found on the Axholme Ancestry site at **www.red1st.com**.

For Nottingham, a genealogical data site at **www.btinternet.com/ ~nttsue/GenealogicalData.htm** carries lists of sheriffs, burgesses, mayors, and other resources transcribed from *Old and New Nottingham* by William Howie Wylie in 1853. The city's lace making industry is explored at **www.bbc.co.uk/legacies/work/england/nottingham/article_1.shtml**, whilst the story of Nottingham lace makers who settled in Calais and then emigrated to Australia in 1848 is detailed by the Australian Society of the Lacemakers of Calais at **www.angelfire.com/al/aslc**. An exploration of the area around Nottingham's western districts and parishes can be explored at **www.broxtowehundred.co.uk/views.htm**.

Material for Mansfield can be found at **http://web.ukonline.co.uk/ lost-mansfield**, including newspaper extracts, copyhold land survey records from the early seventeenth century and constables' records from the 1730s, whilst additional images and memories from people in the area have been recorded at **www.old-mansfield.org.uk**. For people from across Nottinghamshire who were found recorded in the parish registers of Calverton, Lambley, Oxton, Thurgaton and Tithby there is a marriage strays index at **http://tinyurl.com/ykd322g**, as well as register entries from over twenty parishes, a wills strays index and some marriage licenses.

Guy Etchells' site at **http://freespace.virgin.net/guy.etchells** has parish register transcripts for Lenton, Elton-on-the-Hill, Elston, Bingham and Hickling, as well as *A General View of the Agriculture of the County of Nottingham*, by Robert Lowe from 1798. Norton Cuckney is covered at **http://tinyurl.com/yh5bnez**, with various photos, records of baptisms, marriages and burials, and extracts from White's Directory from 1832 and 1864. Parish records for Beeston are also available at **www.beeston-notts. co.uk**, along with an interesting memoir and diary by Sergeant William Jowett of the 7th Royal Fusiliers, published in 1856, which concerns his time at the Crimea. For the village of Bunny, **www.bunnyvillage.org. uk** contains baptisms (1715–1899), marriages (1556–1899) and burials (1715–1899) amongst its offerings.

A one place study for Normanton-on-Soar is available at **http://free pages.genealogy.rootsweb.ancestry.com/~lesleydonald**, with various records for both the village and adjacent parishes. The Ashfield Cemetery Records Online site at **www.ashfield-dc.gov.uk/ashfieldcemeteries/ intro.php?set=yes** has records from six local cemeteries, and for Hucknall Huthwaite, the **www.hucknall-huthwaite.org** site contains gazetteer entries and a press archive from 1676–1982.

Finally, a website dedicated to Warsop Vale in the north of the county is online at **www.warsopvale.org**, containing many historic photos and maps for the area throughout its history as a colliery-based village.

Oxfordshire
A list of Oxfordshire-based parishes and villages is located at **www. ontaworld.co.uk/england/oxfordshire/index.html**, with an interactive parish map for the county provided by the Oxfordshire Family History Society at **www.ofhs.org.uk**. This not only helps you to identify parish locations, but also to identify how many records have been recorded by the society for each parish, which can be accessed through its search

service. The site also offers monumental inscription indexes, and a wills index naming every person noted within more than 30,000 probate documents, sourced both locally and from the Prerogative Court of Canterbury. For identifying historic locations in the county, Smith's *New Map of the County of Oxford* (1801) is at **www.archivemaps.com/mapco/oxford/oxford.htm**.

A look-up exchange for Oxfordshire parish records and other material exists at **www.angelfire.com/wa3/wks/oxon.html**, with a surname interest list online at **www.oxsil.org.uk**. Monumental inscriptions can be found at **www.oxfordinscriptions.com**, and for a glimpse of Oxfordshire churches, you can take your pick from three sites on the subject, located at **www.allthecotswolds.com**, **www.oxfordshirechurches.info** and **http://tinyurl.com/ygr3pf2**.

Hearth tax returns from 1662 for the hundred of Ploughley are at **www.whipple.org/oxford**, along with transcriptions from Oxford arch-deaconry's marriages bonds from 1634–1850. Also within Ploughley, the inhabitants of the parish of Kirtlington in 1723 and 1753 are listed at **www.burrell-wood.org.uk/LHist/Places/Kirtlington/index.htm**, the names having been sourced from local manorial records. For a brief history of Oxford city, visit **www.oxfordcity.co.uk/info/history.html**.

The parish church site for Noke (**http://home.btconnect.com/stgiles_noke**) has register transcriptions, probate records, censuses and hearth tax returns. Headington is catered for at **www.headington.org.uk**, with censuses, directories, maps, school log books, press cuttings and a time-line, whilst Deddington's site at **www.deddington.org.uk** is packed with maps, a workhouse history and more.

Finally for Oxfordshire, an excellent guide to the locations of NHS records from the county, including a list of hospitals, can be found at **www.oxfordshirehealtharchives.nhs.uk**.

Rutland

The smallest of the historic English counties, Rutland only has two towns, Oakham and Uppingham, and today exists as a single unitary authority. Many resources for the county are found in surrounding adjacent counties, in particular Leicestershire. The Leicestershire, Leicester and Rutland Record Office catalogue can be found online at **http://record-office-catalogue.leics.gov.uk/DServe**, whilst a list of the office's parish register holdings, including Rutland, is available at **http://tinyurl.com/yh3sy4r**. The Leicester and Rutland Churches site at **www.leicestershirechurches.co.uk** also covers the county.

The 1851 census for Uppingham has been transcribed and made available through the Rutland Online site at **www.rutnet.co.uk/pp/page/ detail.asp?id=81**, accompanied by details of local historic attractions. A useful guide for researching properties in the town exists at **www.rutnet. co.uk/pp/gold/viewGold.asp?IDType=Page&ID=12820**, as collated by the local studies group. A history of Exton village is at **www.rutnet. co.uk/exton**, whilst a feast of transcribed resources for the village of Langham is available at **www.langhamvillage.com**, including maps, manor court rolls, parish registers and censuses. The PDF documents for the 1841–1881 censuses were unfortunately found to be corrupted at the time of writing, although those for 1891 and 1901 still worked.

The *Leicestershire and Rutland People Index* is worth consulting at **http:// members.multimania.co.uk/larpindex/home.php**, containing details of soldiers, convicts and paupers from the county as found in documents at TNA and elsewhere. Finally, a comprehensive site on the county's war memorials is available at **www.users.globalnet.co.uk/~shelvey**.

Shropshire
The county of Shropshire (also known as 'Salop') on the Welsh marches is one of the least populated English counties. The Discovering Shropshire's History site at **www.discovershropshire.org.uk/html** provides a useful gateway to various county-based sites and resources, and for the lay of the land, a county wide map can also be consulted at **www. jlb2005.plus.com/wales/tallis/maps/sal.htm**, dating approximately to 1850.

Shropshire Archives has an online catalogue at **http://archives. shropshire.gov.uk**, whilst a list of parishes and villages in the county is found at **www.ontaworld.co.uk/england/shropshire/index.html**, though at the time of writing only the parish of Acton Burnell can be further explored via a link on the site. Shropshire Family History Society's website at **www.sfhs.org.uk/resources_menu.asp** has some useful resources online, in the form of a strays index for those appearing in marriages and wills outside of the county, and a monumental inscription surname index. The Joiner Marriage Index at **www.joinermarriageindex.com** carries nearly 50,000 marriages for 106 Shropshire parishes.

The Old Lydbury website (**www.old-lydbury.org.uk**) has directories for the village from 1851–1895, and censuses from 1841–1901, with the exception of 1881. Parish registers for Aleveley are available at **www. sheridansweep.freeserve.co.uk**, with several lists of people in the village at various periods between 1831 and the 1950s.

Historic Ironbridge can be explored at **www.ironbridge.org.uk/about_ us/library_and_archives**, with the site carrying details on extensive collections held at the local museum, historic photographs and information on the various archaeological projects in the vicinity. The history of Madeley is covered at **www.madeleylocalhistory.org**, and Broseley at **www.broseley.org.uk**, with the latter including trade directories, tithe maps and more. Maesbury village is equally well served at **www. maesbury.org** with censuses and other records.

For Shropshire's fallen in the various British conflicts, a Virtual War memorial site at **www.shropshirewarmemorial.org.uk/War_Graves. htm** commemorates almost 7000 soldiers.

Finally for Shropshire, the National Library of Wales' *Crime and Punishment* database at **www.llgc.org.uk/sesiwn_fawr/index_s.htm** includes details of some Shropshire felons.

Somerset

If you have ancestors from Somerset you are particularly fortunate, as there is a wealth of online material to help with your research. The county's record office website at **www1.somerset.gov.uk/archives** is a good starting point, with a catalogue of holdings, the *Somerset Voices* and *Exmoor Oral History* projects, as well as many digitised maps and pictures. Photos from 62 Somerset churches can be viewed at **www. allthecotswolds.com**.

The county's best offerings lie however within the wealth of sources for parish records. A volunteer-based Online Parish Clerk exists at **http:// wsom-opc.org.uk/index.php**, which covers Bristol as well as Somerset, and offers records and links to useful sites for each parish. The *South West England Genealogical Indexes* site at **www.paulhyb.homecall.co.uk** is equally useful, with many parish register transcriptions for areas such as Bridgwater and Taunton, but also Somerset trade directories and newspaper records. Taunton is also served at **www.parkhouse.org.uk**, with parish registers, a Somerset Book of Honour (for the First World War), and monumental inscriptions for St Mary Magdelen's in the town. If your ancestors were from the Weston-Super-Mare area, the local family history society has indexes to baptisms, marriages and burials, as well as images of churches, at **www.wsmfhs.org.uk**. For parishes around Cheddar and Wookey, there are register entries at **www.durtnall. org.uk/Somerset%20Pages.htm**, and for parishes within the hundred of Frome, visit **www.gomezsmart.myzen.co.uk** and **http://fromeresearch. org.uk**. For the parish of Nynehead, visit **www.nynehead.org**.

Several Somerset parishes are dealt with at **http://tinyurl.com/yfq4e36**, whilst Paul Kenyon's site (**www.pbenyon1.plus.com**) hosts additional register transcripts and miscellaneous records. For West Somerset, there is again excellent coverage at Martin Southwood's **www.wsom.org. uk/Parreg.html**. The south east is dealt with by the West Country Genealogy site at **www.westcountrygenealogy.com**, with both parish register and directory listings, and further transcriptions for the south of the county can be found at Sarah Hawkins' excellent **http://freepages. genealogy.rootsweb.ancestry.com/~sarahhawkins**. Records from ten further parishes, including those around Glastonbury, have been placed online at **http://tinyurl.com/yjjjp7b**, mainly from the nineteenth century.

The Winsham Web Museum at **www.winshamwebmuseum.co.uk** is an extremely detailed site with parish records from 1559–1885, burial records for St Stephen's and Winsham cemeteries, and the impressive *Winsham Archive*, containing many miscellaneous records sets from land sales and other document examples. Kingweston village is covered at **http://kingweston.atspace.com**, and Wedmore is served at **www.tutton. org** with parish records from 1561–1860, and other resources such as the *Wedmore Chronicles* from 1898.

Records for Nailsea can be found at **http://myweb.tiscali.co.uk/ ian.sage/Nailsea/nailsea.html**, including war memorial information. Parish entries for Clevedon, along with census material, are online at **www.clevedon-civic-society.org.uk**. For High Littleton and Hallatrow parish records visit **www.highlittletonhistory.org.uk**, and for Timsbury, directories and census records are located at **www.timsbury.net**.

For statutory records in the vicinity of Bath and north east Somerset, an index can be found at the Bath BMD site (**http://bathbmd.org.uk**), which can be used to order up post 1837 certificates from the local register office. Newspaper extracts from the *Bath Chronicle* are hosted on-line through a *Georgian Newspaper Project* at **http://tinyurl.com/ykuyvxz** covering the period from 1770–1800, whilst some further useful resources for Bath, Freshford and Hinton Charterhouse, including images and potted histories, can be found at **www.freshford.com**.

Staffordshire

Images from the historic Staffordshire's past can be viewed on the *Strolling Through Staffordshire* site at **www.thornber.org**, whilst historic maps and essays on a range of historical themes from the county can be viewed at **www.staffspasttrack.org.uk**. The Staffordshire Encyclopaedia site at **www.the-staffordshire-encyclopaedia.co.uk** also provides an excellent range of resources including church memorials, lists of mayors, best kept village competition winners, witches and all sorts, though is slightly marred by a staggering amount of Viagra ads in the comments boxes!

Locally held statutory birth, marriage and death certificates for Staffordshire can be ordered from the various county-based register offices using the Staffordshire BMD site at **www.staffordshirebmd. org.uk**. An equally useful resource is the Staffordshire and Stoke on Trent Archive Service run *Staffordshire Name Indexes* database at **www. staffsnameindexes.org.uk**, which contains a *Calendar of Prisoners at Staffordshire Quarter Sessions Index* (1779–1880), a *Staffordshire Police Force Registers Index* (1842–1920) and a *Diocese of Lichfield and Coventry Wills Index* (1650–1700), with a database on *Workhouse Admissions and Discharges* (1834–1900) well underway. A searchable catalogue for all archives and museums in the Black Country can be further consulted at **www.blackcountryhistory.org**, whilst the Black Country Connections surname interests site at **http://bcconnections.tribalpages.com** can help to make connections. Burials and crematoria records for the modern metropolitan borough of Dudley can be searched freely at **http:// tinyurl.com/yzgu9n4**.

A list of Staffordshire parishes is available at **www.ontaworld.co.uk/ england/staffordshire/index.html** with links to a handful of parish sites providing further information, whilst various parish registers from across the county, in addition to a large Excel file-based *Staffordshire Calendar of Prisoners*, can be found at **http://uk-transcriptions.accessgenealogy. com/Staffs.htm**. The subscription-based **www.midlandshistoricaldata. org** also offers a great deal of material in the form of censuses, directories, books for Staffordshire and other resources for the Midlands counties.

A catalogue for The Sutherland Papers, a massive archive of papers for the Leveson-Gower family, Marquesses of Stafford and Dukes of Sutherland for their estates in the county can be consulted at **www. sutherlandcollection.org.uk**, and handily includes a personal names index.

For Sedgley, a comprehensive research guide, with various photographs, essays and records, can be viewed at **www.sedgleymanor.com**, and includes additional resources for the county such as the *Black Country Dialect Dictionary*. The town of Willenhall is covered on two separate sites, with a list of families in 1532, hearth tax records from 1666, several directories and war memorials available at **http://freespace.virgin.net/**

willen.hall/Willenhall.html. A series of essays on aspects of the town's history, such as cholera outbreaks and its existence in World War Two, can be read at **www.shercliff.demon.co.uk/whs2008**.

Trade directories, censuses and maps for Whittington are online at **www.whittingtonhistorysociety.org.uk**, whilst records for Hints and Canwell in the south of the county are at **www.hints-village.com**. Wills, parish records, manor court records, quarter sessions records and more for Hollinsclough are at **www.hollinsclough.org.uk/localhistory. htm**. Parish records for the village of Betley (1538–1812) can be consulted at **www.betley.net**, along with wills from 1518 onwards, estate sales, and population data from 1086AD.

Census indexes, images, and databases on churches and records for Walsall can help at **www.walsall.gov.uk/localhistorycentre**, with the site also hosting an *Asian Heritage Project*. Walsall's Leather Museum site at **www.walsall.gov.uk/leisure_and_culture/leathermuseum** provides some useful information on a once important occupation within the area.

Commemorating the South Staffordshire Home Guard. Courtesy of Chris Myers

The website for Wolverhampton Archives and Local Studies (**www. wolverhampton.gov.uk/leisure_culture/libraries/archives**), hosts parish registers for Wednesfield, Bliston, Wolverhampton and Willenhall, along with maps identifying the locations of Roman Catholic and nonconformist churches. Images and essays on the history of Wolverhampton can be found at **www.wolverhamptonhistory.org.uk**, whilst war memorials for the city can be found at **www.wolverhamptonwarmemorials.org. uk**. Memorials for Staffordshire's largest city, Stoke-on-Trent, can also be viewed at **http://tinyurl.com/yfemecn**. An interesting site for those who served in the Home Guard in the county from 1940–1944 is also worth exploring at **www.staffshomeguard.co.uk**.

On the occupation front, some additional resources include a site on the 1895 Diglake Colliery Disaster at **www.warrinerprimaries.com/ Topic/diglake.htm**, and a report into child labour within Staffordshire potteries at **www.staffs.ac.uk/schools/humanities_and_soc_sciences/ census/sc1.htm**.

Suffolk
The East Anglian county of Suffolk has produced many famous personalities across the centuries, from the painter John Constable to the Witchfinder General Matthew Hopkins. A list of the county's parishes can be found at the Suffolk Parish registers Index site at **www.rootsweb. ancestry.com/~engdorse/PRSU.html**, with links to some transcribed parish records, whilst a list of registers microfilmed and made available for viewing or purchase from Suffolk Record Office can be examined at **http://tinyurl.com/yk3pzu4**. Images from most of the county's churches are available to view at **www.suffolkchurches.co.uk**.

Stowmarket's history is recorded at **www.stowmarket-history.co. uk**, and includes parish registers, monumental inscriptions and other records. For Woolpit, registers can be found at **http://tinyurl.com/ yh3wc4w**, though the year range is not listed, and for Haverhill, visit **www.haverhill-uk.com/pages/genealogy-home-134.htm**. Records for Beaumont Baptist Church and Quay United Reformed Church in Woodbridge can be found at **www.woodbridgechurch.org.uk**.

A guide to researching records for the village of Debenham can be found at **www.debenhamfamilyhistory.org.uk**, as well as information from war memorials, wills indexes and more. The history of Elmswell is recorded at **www.elmswell-history.org.uk** whilst Freston is covered at **http://wanborough.ukuhost.co.uk/Freston.htm**, with online resources including census indexes.

On the newspaper front, extracts from the *Suffolk and Essex Free Press*, *Haverhill Echo* and *Suffolk Free Press* are available at **www.foxearth.org. uk/newspapers.html**, whilst details of articles and publications from the Suffolk Record Society are hosted at **www.suffolkrecordssociety.com**, from where copies can be purchased.

Surrey
First recorded as 'Sudrigean' in Saxon times, the historic county of Surrey is located near London in the south-east. As such, many resources for the county are also found within those outlined earlier for Greater London (see p. 91).

The Surrey History Centre site at **www.surreycc.gov.uk/surrey historyservice** includes guides to the county's parish records, as well as information on the Queen's Royal Surrey Regiment. The *Surrey Plus* wills index, which covers Surrey and nine neighbouring counties, is also online at **www.rootsweb.ancestry.com/~engsurry**, with additional wills from the Archdeaconry Court of Surrey wills and Commissary Court available at the Origins Network. An index to Surrey Advertiser articles from 1864–67 and 1872 is online at **www.newspaperdetectives. co.uk**, whilst several Hampshire and Surrey titles are indexed at **http:// freespace.virgin.net/anglers.rest/surreyhants.htm**.

A detailed map for Surrey from 1768 can be found at **www.rootsweb. ancestry.com/~engsurry/maps/roque.html**. For the east of the county, the relevant family history society has several free to use databases at **www.eastsurreyfhs.org.uk/free2view/f2vindex.html**, such as Caterham Asylum wages books, school rolls of honour, Croydon Wesleyan and Congregational parish records, Camberwell apprentices, and more. The *Research Croydon* catalogue, for holdings of the local archive, local studies library and museum, is also available at **www.croydon.gov.uk/ leisure/archives/rsdatabase**. The Epsom and Ewell History Explorer site (**www.epsomandewellhistoryexplorer.org.uk**) has a remarkable collection of essays and photos on a variety of topics from the area, whilst Redhill and Reigate are covered at **www.redhill-reigate-history. co.uk** with maps, photos and resources on the home guard, lists of mayors, and other materials. Census transcriptions for the village of Buckland are online at **www.bucklandsurrey.net**, as well as a history of the local school, and history resources for Leatherhead at **www.leatherheadweb. org.uk**.

There are several useful resources for Kingston upon Thames. The local museum at **www.kingston.gov.uk/leisure/museum** contains online guides such as *Kingston at War* and *Kingston's Royal Connections*, whilst historical statutory birth and marriage indexes can be accessed at **http://tinyurl.com/yle62n2**. The Kingston University Life Cycles site at **http://tinyurl.com/yhtelg3** hosts censuses from 1851–91, Bonner Hill Cemetery burial registers from 1855–1911, and parish marriage and burial registers from 1850–1901.

For Richmond upon Thames, the Local History and Heritage site at **http://tinyurl.com/yzczmwu** contains guides to people of historical note buried in the borough (separated into two files, A-L and M-Z), Victoria Cross holders, and various timelines. A community archives site at **www2.richmond.gov.uk/communityarchive** contains old photos, whilst burials from Richmond can be researched at **www2.richmond.gov.uk/ burials**. A downloadable guide to Lambeth's archives holdings can be consulted at **http://tinyurl.com/yj5gu6o**, whilst a database of all resold and reused graves in West Norwood Cemetery is available at **www. lambeth.gov.uk/cemetery**. A list of men from Addlestone who fell in the Great War is online at **www.freewebs.com/addlestonegreatwardead**, with detailed biographies of many. For Surrey policemen who died in the same war visit **www.thinblueline.org.uk** (the site also caters for Sussex).

In the west of the county, a list of pay-to-view research guides, images of churches and a free to view 1837 parish map can be consulted at **www.wsfhs.org**. A one place study for Puttenham at **http://freespace. virgin.net/ar.indexes/puttenham.htm** includes parish records, an index of PCC will entries, bastardy papers, constable records, and several family pedigrees from the area. Records for Wyke, Christmaspie, Willey Green, Pinewood and Flexford (within the parish of Normandy) can be found at **http://normandyhistorians.co.uk**, and the village of Bisley is well catered for at **www.rootsweb.ancestry.com/~engsurry/bisley**, with parish records, militia musters, lords of the manor, lay subsidies 1585–1649, nonconformist records and more.

Finally for the county, the Surrey Vintage Vehicle Society hosts an interesting site at **www.svvs.org/help10.shtml** which can help you to identify vintage cars from old photos.

Sussex

Sussex has an excellent Online Parish Clerks site at **www.sussex-opc. org** which includes parish registers databases, protestation returns and poll registers, as well as an interesting project allowing searches for Sussex folk found within the London, Edinburgh and Belfast Gazettes.

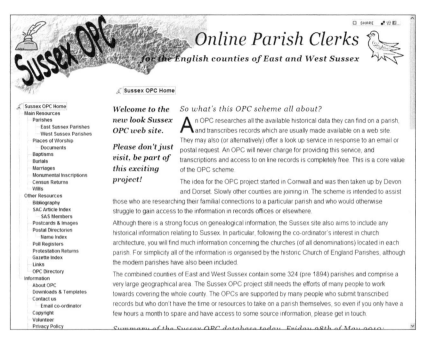

The foremost online repository of Sussex records. Courtesy of the Sussex OPC Scheme

The county's family history society site at **www.sfhg.org.uk** has some equally handy parish resources, back issues of the *Sussex Links* newsletters from 2002–2010, a Sussex marriage strays database and more. West Sussex Record Office has a searchable catalogue online at **www.westsussexpast.org.uk/searchonline** which lists its holdings.

The *Ye Olde Sussex* project at **www.yeoldesussexpages.com** has several interesting essays on various aspects of the county's past, such as the history of smuggling, gaols, banks, castles, folklore, architecture and more. The Weald of Kent, Surrey and Sussex website (**http://weald.org**) carries many pedigrees, images, digitised books and maps, whilst further maps from 1575–1900 can be sourced from **http://tinyurl.com/yjpjh7d**. The Sussex Records Society (**www.sussexrecordsociety.org.uk**) hosts twelve records databases including apprentices and masters, lay subsidy rolls 1524–25, the 1747 Window Tax and others. Kelly's 1867 county directory is online at **http://steve.pickthall.users.btopenworld.com/ssx1867/kellys1867.html**.

The 1066 Genealogy site at **http://tinyurl.com/yjnrfqm** for Hastings and Lewes has census and parish records, but also interesting items such as discussions on Martello Towers and more. For Fishbourne, a one place study at **http://steve.pickthall.users.btopenworld.com/nfops/ index.html** includes parish registers, census entries and directories, whilst records for Portslade can be consulted at **www.stnicolas. standrewportslade. btinternet.co.uk**.

Records for Broadhurst and Worthing can be found at **www. barriesgenealogy.co.uk**, for Fernhurst at **www.fernhurstsociety.org. uk/genealogy/cen_intro.html** (mainly census material) and for Ringmer at **www.ringmer.info**. A tithe map for Barcombe and Hamsey is available at **www.bandhpast.co.uk**, along with additional maps and the 1841 census, whilst the Cuckfield Compendium (**www.cuckfield compendium.co.uk**) has everything bar the kitchen sink with parish records, local ghost stories, quarter session material and war memorials. Various burials from Bexhill, Brighton, Halton, Hastings, Salehurst, Shoreham and many other Sussex based cemeteries can be found at **www.genealogylinks.net/uk/england/sussex/cemeteries.htm**. A look up exchange at **http://homepage.ntlworld.com/w.jowett/sussexlookup. html** provides offers of help for directories, parish records, census entries and more from many other parishes.

Further sites of interest include the Brighton and Hove photo-graphers' studios index at **www.spartacus.schoolnet.co.uk/DSindex. htm**, and the previously mentioned **www.thinblueline.org.uk** which commemorates both Sussex and Surrey police men who lost their lives in the Great War.

Warwickshire (and Birmingham)
The volunteer-based Warwickshire Online Parish Clerk site at **www. hunimex.com/warwick/opc/opc.html** is a useful gateway to many on-line collections of records for both the county and Birmingham.

Warwickshire County Council has a fantastic assortment of resources online through its site at **www.warwickshire.gov.uk/registration**, such as its post 1837 indexes to locally held statutory records for birth, marriages and deaths. The county record office site at **http://tinyurl. com/ybn7r2u** contains an online catalogue entitled *Warwickshire's Past Unlocked*, which is updated every three months, and a *Calendars of Prisoners* database listing people held in the county prisons at Warwick, Birmingham and Coventry as they awaited trial at the Courts of Assize and at the Quarter Sessions courts in Warwick between 1800 and 1900. The site also has a *Licensed Victuallers* database for 1801–1828, with information sourced from the calendars of Victuallers' Recognizances held in the county's quarter sessions records, and a *Tithe Apportionments* database produced in 1836. The *Windows on Warwickshire* site (**www. windowsonwarwickshire.org.uk**) carries historic county photos and images.

The excellent Pickard's Pink Pages for Warwickshire at **www. hunimex.com/warwick** carries free to access census, directory, BMD and miscellaneous records for the whole county, such as lists of Warwickshire freeholders, Coventry-based freemen, apprentices, and more. A 1670 Hearth Tax list is also available at **www.hunimex.com/warwick/census/ hearth_1670.html**. The subscription-based **www.midlandshistoricaldata. org** includes many useful sets of records such as twentieth century electoral rolls for Birmingham and Warwickshire Poor Law records.

The Birmingham and Midland Society for Genealogy and Heraldry (**www.bmsgh.org**) has several online research guides for Warwickshire and Birmingham, and a listing of society held publications in its library. The Nuneaton and North Warwickshire site at **www.nnwfhs.org.uk** includes a parish map from 1871, a photo gallery and downloadable quarterly society journal back issues from 1995–2007

Specifically for Birmingham, the Archives and Heritage portal at **www.birmingham.gov.uk/archivesandheritage** includes some valuable resources, such as a *Black History Collection*, maps and lists of famous people from Birmingham. The Birmingham Heritage site (**www. birminghamheritage.org.uk**) is useful for information on various historic institutions in the city.

Coventry Family History Society has placed some material at **www. covfhs.org.uk**, including transcripts from Lascelle's 1851 directory, a list of canal boats from 1879–1936 (sourced from the Coventry Canal Register of Boats), and a convicts register for 1879 and 1890–97. The city's experience in the Blitz is outlined at **www.familyresearcher. co.uk**.

The University of Warwick's Coventry-based Modern Records Centre at **www2.warwick.ac.uk/services/library/mrc** has online galleries of images themed around subjects as diverse as the Cold War, Trade Unions history and Freedom and Liberty, and carries guides for researching the county's social, economic and political history. (The site is also accessible at **http://modernrecords.warwick.ac.uk**). For the

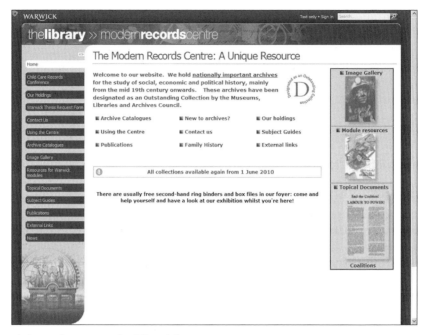

A feast of resources for Warwick. Courtesy of Modern Records Centre, University of Warwick

history of the Midlands in the Industrial Revolution from 1700–1830 you can visit **www.revolutionaryplayers.org.uk**, which hosts a digital library.

Shakespeare's home of Stratford upon Avon is explored at **www. shakespeare.org.uk/content/view/543/504**, and includes a burials database (1881–1964), a police charge book (1863–1880), workhouse records and even a smallpox census from 1765. Wendy Boland's free look-ups site at **http://uk-transcriptions.accessgenealogy.com/Wendy's%20lookups. htm** is useful for those with ancestry in Birdingbury, Newbold on Avon, Dunchurch, Grandborough, Frankton and Preston Bagot, and contains census entries from 1841 and 1891.

A village site for Lighthorne at **www.lighthorneonline.com/VHHome. htm** has records for the 1881 and 1901 censuses, the local war memorial and its school. Various aspects of Solihull's history are featured, along with maps, at **www.solihull-online.com/history.htm**, whilst the history of Oxhill is explored at **www.oxhill.org.uk**, including some parish and land records. Elsewhere in the county, images from many Warwickshire-based churches have been posted at **www.allthecotswolds.com**.

Finally for the region, the West Midlands Police Museum site at **www. westmidlandspolicemuseum.co.uk** has a detailed history of police forces in the region including those in Birmingham and Coventry.

Westmorland

There are very few standalone resources for Westmorland alone, as the former county is often lumped in with Cumberland (see p. 66) as part of modern Cumbria. The Cumberland and Westmorland Archives site at **www.cumberlandarchives.co.uk** include parish registers and an 1873 directory, whilst several directories and parish register material can be located at **www.btinternet.com/~grigg**. Westmorland Hearth Tax records from 1674 are available at **http://tinyurl.com/ygxpcql**.

A list of relevant county history publications can be consulted at **www. cumbriafhs.com**, and information on the work behind the Victoria County History for the region is detailed at **www.cumbrialocalhistory. org.uk**.

The Durham Mining Museum project (see p. 49) covers Westmorland, and records from the Cumbrian Manorial Records Project from the University of Lancashire can be examined at **www.lancs.ac.uk/fass/ projects/manorialrecords/index.htm**.

Wiltshire

Wiltshire and Swindon Archive's site at **http://history.wiltshire.gov. uk** carries an online catalogue for its holdings, whilst the council's impressive Wiltshire Wills database at **www.wshc.eu/about-wshc/ archives.209.html** catalogues 105,000 wills from 1540–1858, from the Salisbury Diocese. About a quarter of these have been digitised, and can be consulted upon payment of a fee. As well as Wiltshire, there are some entries for people from Berkshire, Devon and Dorset.

The Wiltshire Web site (**www.wiltshire-web.co.uk/towns_villages. asp**) has a guide to the county's many towns and villages. Whilst there is an Online Parish Clerks site at **www.wiltshire-opc.org.uk**, the coverage is very limited so far, with the site still looking for volunteers for many of the parish pages. Duncan and Mandy Ball's site of 28,000 photos of churches taken in North Wiltshire is worth consulting at **http:// oodwooc.co.uk**, whilst images from 2020 churches in the county are also available at **www.allthecotswolds.com**.

Parish register records from Brinkworth and Dauntsey are available at **www.henly.f9.co.uk/wiltshire.html**, as well as ships money lists, manorial surveys and resources for neighbouring parishes. Dauntsey parish records are also found at the Moonrakers Wiltshire Genealogy site (**www.moonrakers.org.uk**), as well as for Bishoptone, with the project also containing many pedigree and surname lists. Records for Aldbourne (1790–1849) are at **www.treelines.co.uk/OPC/opcintro. html**, whilst baptisms from bishops' transcripts for Donhead St Mary (1622–1810) have been placed at **www.roughwood.net/VitalRecords/ VitalRecordsFrames.htm**.

West Grimstead records can be accessed at **www.westgrimstead familyhistory.co.uk**, including bastardy orders, the 1841–1911 censuses, parish records from 1622–1983 (though most twentieth century records must be applied for by e-mail), Methodist records, a 1918 register of electors and a roll of honour. A list of incumbents for Swindon parish church from 1302–1885 is available at **http://homepages.nildram.co. uk/~Jimella/trnscrpt.htm#wilts**, along with names of people in and around South Marston. If your ancestry lies in Limpley Stoke, visit **www.freshford.com** for various historic images, OS and tithe maps. The site goes into more detail for Bradford on Avon, with records such as poor rates, land tax records, the Duke of Kingston's Survey of 1752 and a rental list from 1550.

For Devizes, workhouse records of births from 1848–1902 and a list of deaths from 1866–1902 can be found at **http://thor.prohosting.com/ ~hughw/Devizesb.txt**.

Two further interesting resources for the county include **www. wbct.org.uk/history** which has a history of Wiltshire and Berkshire Canal Trust, newspaper extracts from the Swindon Advertiser (1860–1910) and some historic documents and images, and **www.thewardrobe. org.uk**, the site of the Rifles (Berkshire and Wiltshire) Museum, which includes 16,500 documents war diary records for 15 battalions of Royal Berkshire and Wiltshire Regiments from 1914–1919.

Worcestershire
For a general introduction to Worcestershire's history, the record office has several online projects and exhibitions at **http://tinyurl.com/ycbpljc**, including a picture gallery, a Victorian Worcestershire display, Black and Asian History sources, a Sound Archive and a World War Two oral history project.

The Worcestershire branch of the Birmingham and Midland Society for Genealogy and Heraldry (**www.worcesterbmsgh.co.uk/Introduction. html**) hosts an online parish records research guide. The information provided includes the identification of a parish by its OS reference and the name of the hundred to which it belongs, the local poor law union, and locations of relevant sets of records. Images from over seventy churches in the county can be viewed at **www.allthecotswolds.com**.

The subscription-based **www.midlandshistoricaldata.org** site contains several resources for the county, whilst miscellaneous resources for Kidderminster, Kings Norton, Dudley and Worcester are freely available at **http://uk-transcriptions.accessgenealogy.com/Worcs.htm**. Parish records for Berrow, Bredon and Chaceley and surrounding parishes are found at **http://freepages.genealogy.rootsweb.ancestry. com/~wrag44/index.htm**.

Malvern Family History Society hosts a bibliography of local history books and monumental inscriptions for Cradley and Mathon at **www. mfhs.org.uk/Local%20History%20Books%20new.html**. Cradley, part of the parish of Halesowen, is further explored at **www.cradleylinks. co.uk**, with pictures, monumental inscriptions, the 1841 census, probate records and a list of surname interests. Halesowen, in fact a part of Shropshire until 1844, is dealt with at **www.halesowenroots.com**, with parish records, directories, maps, rolls of honour and various local family history sites. Historic maps and images of Worcester are hosted by Worcester City Museum at **www.worcestercitymuseums.org.uk/ content/resind.htm**.

For Wythall, a one place study at **http://freepages.history.rootsweb. ancestry.com/~wythallindex/index.htm** has information on almost 20,000 names from the parish's history. Information on Blockley can be found at **http://members.shaw.ca/panthers5/blockley.html**, including directories, censuses, a roll of honour, the Blockley Riot of 1878, maps, monumental inscriptions and wills. Burial records from 1904–2009 for Holy Trinity church of Amblecote are online at **www.holytrinity amblecote.org.uk**, whilst parish records for Badsey from 1530–1909 are available at **www.badsey.net**, along with photos, maps, various essays on aspects of Badsey's history.

On the military front, the regimental site for the Worcestershire Regiment, which dates back to 1694, is located at **www.worcestershire regiment.com** and includes, amongst many things, POW stories and war diaries transcripts from 1944–1945.

Yorkshire

Yorkshire is the largest county in England, bigger than Northern Ireland and just over two thirds the size of Wales. Founded initially as the Roman city of Eboracum, and long recognised by many as 'God's own county', it would be a brave man who told a Yorkshireman otherwise! Due to its size, the white rose county was historically administered as three 'ridings' in the east, north and west.

County-based indexes for statutory birth, marriage and death records from 1837–1950 can be found at the Yorkshire BMD site (**www.yorkshire bmd.org.uk**), and can be used to order up certificates from the various registration offices across the county. The Yorkshire Indexers subscription site (**www.yorkshireindexers.co.uk**) costs £10 a year for unlimited access to monumental inscription records, burial records, the 1937 Leeds Register of Electors, and more, as well as a discussion forum (other subscriptions are available). Several oral history projects have been recorded at **www.myyorkshire.org**, which includes many images and stories from the participants. A guide to printed Yorkshire newspaper indexes and their locations is listed at **www.yli.org.uk/ newsplan/yhindex.htm**.

On the military front, the Prince of Wales Own Regiment of Yorkshire (fourteenth and fifteenth regiments of Foot) are explored at **www. pwo-yorkshire.museum**, whilst the names of civilian war dead from the Second World war are included at **www.genuki.org.uk/big/eng/ Indexes/NE_WarDead** alongside entries from Northumberland and Durham.

The Mormons' free to access FamilySearch Record Search Pilot site at **http://pilot.familysearch.org** carries bishops' transcripts for records from the Diocese of Durham from 1700–1900, which includes records for York, though the database can only be browsed. The history of Yorkshire Quakers is explored at **www.hull.ac.uk/oldlib/archives/quaker/projres. htm** and has lists of meeting houses etc, whilst a University of Leeds project at **www.leeds.ac.uk/library/spcoll/quaker/index.htm** has searchable database of Quaker records.

The City of York, in the north of the county, is home to the Borthwick Institute for Archives, which has a great many records for the county, and a series of online research guides at **www.york.ac.uk/inst/bihr**. The guides cover various subjects such as Churchwardens' accounts, women's history, disability, LGBT history, health archives and more. Its most significant genealogical collection is perhaps the records for the Prerogative Court of York (PCY), the highest probate court in the north of England. These are slowly being indexed with the Exchequer Courts for York and placed online at the Origins Network site, covering 1731–1858 at the time of writing. Other probate sources on the site include the *York Medieval Probate Index* (1267–1500) and the *York Peculiars Probate Index* (1383–1883).

York Castle Prison (**www.yorkcastleprison.org.uk**) has an online database of almost 5000 convicted criminals, debtors and victims, derived mainly from eighteenth century records, whilst the City of York and District Family History Society at **www.yorkfamilyhistory.org.uk/assizes.htm** has a York Assizes database (1785–1851), and a parish list.

The Yorkshire Dales are well covered at **www.dalesgenealogy.com**, with census returns for many parishes, emigrant ships lists, school log books, gravestone photos and more. For Coxwold village, head teachers' log books from the 1860s to the 1970s can be found at **http://coxwold-village.co.uk/default.aspx**. The role of Craven in the Great War is explored at **www.cpgw.org.uk**, whilst various resources for Redmire and Castle Bolton can be found at **www.redmire.net**. The genealogy section of a site focussed on Grewelthorpe at **www.grewelthorpe.org.uk** has details of many families from the village, and census records for Gunnerside are online at **www.gunnerside.info**. Knaresborough's history is detailed at **www.knaresborough.co.uk/history**, whilst resources for Kirby Misperton going back to the Domesday Book can be consulted at **www.kirbymisperton.org.uk**. The industrial and social history of Langcliffe is explored at **www.langcliffe.net**, whilst the whole of North Yorkshire is included in the Durham Mining Museum website (see p. X). Bob Sanders offers North Yorkshire census look-ups at **www.glamorganfamilyhistory.co.uk/maritime/WHITIND.html**, with the site also acting as an excellent gateway to other resources compiled by many volunteers, notably for Whitby, Scarborough and the moors.

In the east of the county, a comprehensive guide to the censuses taken from 1801–2011 is available at the East of Yorkshire Family History Society website at **www.eyfhs.org.uk**. The catalogue for the East Riding Archives based at Beverley can be viewed at **http://tinyurl.com/3xxdjsn**.

The city of Hull's museum service has a resources catalogue at **www.hullcc.gov.uk/museumcollections**, whilst the Hull History Centre has a catalogue at **http://lib3.adir.hull.ac.uk/dserve**. For Hull's maritime history, the crews of the SS *Canada* and SS *New Zealand*, two fishing boats from the city, are currently being examined at the Hull Trawler Challenge site at **www.whatsthatpicture.com/hull-trawler-challenge**.

Pocklington's local history group's site at **www.pocklingtonhistory. com** has many resources in its Archives section, including maps, church records and more.

An online catalogue at **www.archives.wyjs.org.uk** for the West of Yorkshire Archives Service lists various holdings, whilst the archive's *Tracks in Time: the Leeds Tithe Map Project* at **www.tracksintime.wyjs. org.uk** explores the urban and rural townships of Leeds from 1838– 1861, with apportionment data for the city and digitised tithes maps which can be compared to modern Ordnance Survey resources. The Leeds Library and Information Service site (**www.leedslocalindex.net**) hosts many databases, including Leeds and Yorkshire-based news cuttings, a local biographical index, parish, nonconformist and Quaker registers, and various census resources. The names of 50,000 absent voters over the age of 21 from the 1914–1918 electoral rolls are search-able at **http://tinyurl.com/yg9kyqs**. Most were absent due to military service, and may well have been serving with the Leeds Rifles – if so,

The Leeds Tithe Map Project. Couresy of West Yorkshire Archive Service supported by HLF

the regimental site at **www.yorkshirevolunteers.org.uk/leedsrifles.htm** may also be of interest. A photographic archive for the city is online at **www.leodis.org**.

The Court Rolls of the Manor of Wakefield from 1274–1297 can be found at **http://tinyurl.com/yh4cag9**, whilst a timeline for Bradford's history from 1066–1999 is at **www.bradfordtimeline.co.uk**. The Huddersfield and District Family History Society site at **www.hdfhs. org.uk** has a list of townships and parish descriptions from an 1834 directory, and many useful resource lists.

The village of Brotherton website (**www.brotherton.org.uk**) hosts many family pedigrees, as well as some war memorial and census information. For Todmorden and Walsden, **http://todmordenandwalsden. co.uk** hosts monumental inscriptions, parish records, the censuses from 1841–1901, and parish relief records. The *From Weaver to Web* site at **www.calderdale.gov.uk/wtw** has an online visual archive of Calderdale's history which also includes resources for Todmorden, as well as Halifax, Brighouse, Elland, Hebden Bridge and Sowerby Bridge. Calverly is explored at **www.calverley.info/cal_home.htm**, with a vital record and censuses database, war memorial information, directories and a 1770 parish map, as well as holding records for surrounding villages. Materials for Gisburn village, including burial records (1558–2007) can be found at **www.gisburn.org.uk**, whilst a roll of honour for Haworth is just one of the resources at **www.haworth-village.org.uk**. The **www.kirkheatononlineparishclerk.com** site has a Huddersfield absent voters list from 1918, burials, hearth tax returns, wills extracts and monumental inscriptions.

In the south, Sheffield's family history society site at **www.sheffield fhs.org.uk** offers many resources including censuses, a Sheffield and Hallam Bank register, a released prisoners index from 1858–72, parish records, and many regionally-based research guides. The Sheffield Indexers (**www.sheffieldindexers.com**) host many free to access parish records, the 1841 census, school admission registers, directories and institutions, a statutory births, marriages and deaths certificate project, and a discussion forum. Similar resources can also be found at **www. sheffieldrecordsonline.org.uk**, whilst a Sheffield Cemetery database can be searched at **www.gencem.org**. The biggest peacetime disaster in Victorian Britain is often claimed to be the Sheffield Flood of March 1864, when the Dale Dyke breached, and Mick Hartfield's excellent website, *The Great Flood at Sheffield*, gives unparalleled coverage of the event at **http://mick-armitage.staff.shef.ac.uk/sheffield/flood.html**. Many images from the disaster, one of the first to be photographed in Britain, are online at **www.picturesheffield.co.uk/about.html**, a site from the Sheffield Library Service which hosts some 35,000 historic images from the city's past.

The effects of the 1864 flood at Rotherham are also covered online at **www.rotherhamweb.co.uk/h/extracts/flood.htm**, with many newspaper reports and other contemporary materials. The wider history of Rotherham is covered at **www.rotherhamunofficial.co.uk**, with the site including borough and town maps. The Rotherham Family History Society site (**www.rotherhamfhs.co.uk**) has an Anglican parish map, a list of mayors from 1871, a list of feoffees (trustees) of common lands of Rotherham, and a guide to the area's churches.

An indexing project for Barnsley at **www.barnsleyfhs.co.uk** is catering for the locally held statutory records from 1837 for the region, whilst **www.barnsley.gov.uk** has Barnsley Archives' baptism database, records from Elsecar Congregational Church from 1871–1880, a database of names drawn from John Burland's *Annals of Barnsley and it's Environs 1744–1864*, and a wills and probate database. For Barnsley burials, visit **www.cemeteries.org.uk**.

Information on churches and records in the district surrounding Doncaster can be found at **www.doncasterfhs.co.uk**, whilst research and subject guides for the city are available at **www.doncaster.gov.uk/localstudies**. For Tickhill resources visit **www.tickhillhistorysociety.org.uk**. Finally for the south, a fascinating site entitled the *South Yorkshire Historic Environment Characterisation* can be viewed at **www.sytimescapes.org.uk** which shows how the use of land has changed in the region from 1400 to the present day, via a colour coded map system.

Chapter Five

WALES

In this chapter we will look at many Welsh offerings on a county basis, but it is first worth flagging up some additional sites specific to Wales that may be of interest.

The brilliant Data Wales (**www.data-wales.co.uk**) is well worth a visit, with some fascinating articles on subjects such as the role of the Welsh in slavery, Welsh surnames, place names, emigration and more. Of particular interest are dedicated pages on specific topics such as the Welsh slate industry and the legacy of industry in the South Wales valleys. Also providing some excellent resources is Gathering the Jewels (Casglu'r Tlysau) at **www.gtj.org.uk**, which hosts over 30,000 images of letters, books, aerial photos and more from various different archives and museums, within dedicated sections on Art and Culture, Health, Welfare and Charity, Education, Industry and War and Rebellion.

The Timeline of Genealogically Interesting Dates at **http://home. clara.net/tirbach/HelpPagepearls6.html#nineteenth** is a chronological list of world events but with a strong Welsh bias. As well as placing various Welsh developments of interest into their world context, the site also provides links from each entry to a website that can further explore the subject matter described. BBC Wales has a family history site at **www.bbc.co.uk/wales/history/sites/themes/family.shtml** which includes a useful article on the subject of the Welsh patronymic naming pattern (Rhys ap Dafydd, Rhys son of David, etc).

Anglesey (Ynys Môn)
Anglesey was once a county in its own right, but now forms part of Gwynedd. The island's record office has a guide to its holdings at

www.anglesey.gov.uk/doc.asp?cat=2667&doc=2545, whilst papers for the island's many estates are actually held at Bangor University Library, which has a searchable catalogue online at **www.bangor.ac.uk/library**. A catalogue for holdings in Anglesey Libraries is also available at **http:// talisprism.talnet.gov.uk**. For an index to articles in *Transactions*, the journal of the Anglesey Antiquarian Society and Field Club, visit **www. hanesmon.org.uk/e107/news.php**.

Indexes for locally registered statutory births, marriages and deaths from 1837 are included in the North Wales BMD site at **www.northwales bmd.org.uk**. A series of Calvinistic and Wesleyan Methodist births and baptismal records can also be found on the GENUKI Anglesey page, from both the Holyhead and Beaumaris circuits.

A gateway site to various heritage resources, including a history, timeline, maritime history and photos of the island's churches, can be found at **www.anglesey.info**. Further historic photos are available at **http://tinyurl.com/yjrsoy3** whilst maps of the island from 1579–1720 can be found at **www.anglesey-history.co.uk/maps/index.html**.

Census and church records for Amlwch, as well as trade directories and information on the local copper mine, can be found at **www. amlwchdata.co.uk**, with further information on the mines available at **www.parysmountain.co.uk**. Records for Llanddaniel can be found online at **www.llanddaniel.co.uk**, whilst the *Reports of the Commissioners of Inquiry into the State of Education in Wales* (1847) has a return for Anglesey at **www.llgc.org.uk/index.php?id=776**. A return of land-owners from 1873 is at **www.cefnpennar.com/ang1873land/index.htm**.

Breconshire (Brecknockshire)

Today, most of the historic county of Breconshire is incorporated within the modern local government county of Powys. A description of the county in the 1868 National Gazetteer is available at **www.genuki.com/ big/wal/BRE/Gaz1868.html**. Powys Heritage Online (**http://history. powys.org.uk**) has a great deal of material on Breconshire, including articles on subjects as diverse as canals, railways, roads, workhouses, religion, and land units. For the history of its churches, visit the *Brecknockshire Churches Survey* pages at **www.cpat.demon.co.uk/projects/ longer/churches/brecon/idxbrec.htm**, the results of a survey carried out in 1995/96 by the Clwyd-Powys Archaeological Trust.

Powys County Archive Office library catalogue is available at **www. powys.gov.uk/index.php?id=647&L=0&** and hosts a detailed guide of holdings – follow the links to Local Studies Sources. An index to articles in *Cronicl Powys*, the journal of the Powys Family History Society, can be found at **http://tinyurl.com/ygo42xc**.

Census entries for Christ College, Brecon (1871–1911), can be found at **www.jlb2005.plus.com/walespic/churches/wfha-breconcensus.htm**. For the history of Hay-on-Wye, the famous book town, visit **www. hay-on-wye.co.uk/info/hayhistory.htm**.

Caernarfonshire (Carnarvonshire)
Now a part of Gwynedd, a description of historic Caernarfonshire from the 1849 *Topographical Dictionary of Wales* is located at **www.welshicons. org.uk/html/caernarvonshire.php**.

The local indexes to statutory birth, marriage and death indexes for the county are included in the North Wales BMD project (**www. northwalesbmd.org.uk**). A list of major holdings at Caernarfon Record Office is online at **http://tinyurl.com/yhpl2be**, with details of the archive's

A key resource for Carnarvon-based trading ancestors. Courtesy of Keith Morris

parish registers online at **www.genuki.com/big/wal/CAE/CAE_PR.html**. The catalogue for Gwynedd Archives, entitled *Rhagorol*, is at **www. gwynedd.gov.uk/gwy_doc.asp?cat=3693&doc=12971&Language=1**. The history of the various communities in Penllyn can be found at **www.penllyn.com/1/Hanes/hanes.htm**. A list of traders extracted from directories and censuses (including the 1794 census for Carnarvon), burials at Llanbeblig (1699–1968) and various biographies, is hosted at **www.carnarvontraders.com**. Rent rolls for Llanbeblig from 1832 and poor relief extracts from 1788 can also be found at **www.cefnpennar.com/carnarvon/index.htm**. A detailed site for the village of Rhiw, including old pictures, history, religion, the 1861–1891 censuses, diaries, estate papers and more, exists at **www.rhiw.com**.

Cardiganshire (Ceredigion)

Now part of Dyfed, information on historic Cardiganshire can be found at the Dyfed Family History Society website (**http://dyfedfhs.org.uk**), which carries many useful lists, such as a guide to the county's parishes, burial sites (with some online indexes), graduates from Oxford University and school records.

A catalogue of Ceredigion Archives' holdings is available at **http://archifdy-ceredigion.org.uk**, whilst a return of landowners from 1873 can be viewed at **www.cefnpennar.com**. A useful miscellany of interesting facts and material relating to several parishes in the county is found at **http://home.clara.net/tirbach/HelpPagepearlsCGN.html**.

An index to the Cardiganshire Constabulary Register of Criminals (1897–1933) is available at **www.genuki.org.uk/big/wal/CGN/CGN Criminals.html**, which can be used to track down original entries on the manuscript which has been digitised and made available at **www.llgc.org.uk/index.php?id=criminals**.

A useful list of nonconformist churches and chapels is also available at **www.genuki.com/big/wal/CGN/CGNchapels.html**. The history of the parish of Llangynfelyn is explored at **www.llangynfelyn.org** and includes census records, parish registers, chapel records, tithe records, maps of the parish and county, old and contemporary photographs and more.

For the history of mining in the county visit **www.spirit-of-the-miners. org.uk**, whilst some recent materials on the Cwmystwyth lead mine and the mines at Llanddewibrefi are available at **http://people.exeter.ac.uk/pfclaugh/mhinf/contents.htm#wales**.

Carmarthenshire
The historic county of Carmarthenshire is also a part of modern
Dyfed. A map of the county in 1885, as drawn up by the Boundary
Commissioners for England and Wales, is available at **www.london
ancestor.com/maps/bc-ycarm-th.htm**, with a parish map accessible at
www.llanegwad-carmarthen.co.uk/carmarthenshireparishesmap.htm.
The county records office has only one useful resource online, in the
form of an excellent school records index at **http://tinyurl.com/yjbsc8c**,
though the Friends of Carmarthen Archives has a series of articles
concerning various aspects of the county's history at **www.carmarthen
museum.org.uk**. A series of online reprints of journals by Carmarthenshire Community Council's Local History Committee (1961–1985) is
available at the *Carmarthen Historian* site at **http://carmarthenshire
historian.org**. For a database on place names and estate maps from the
county visit Carmarthenshire Antiquarian Society at **www.carmants.
org.uk**, whilst a report on the hundreds, parishes and schools of
Carmarthenshire can be consulted at **http://tinyurl.com/yfhgd6n**. Online
resources at Dyfed FHS equally apply to Carmarthenshire (see p. 126).
A history of Kidwelly, with articles, directory records, the 1901
census, images, maps, rental rolls, and more can be consulted at
www.kidwellyhistory.co.uk. For the parish of Llangewad visit **www.
llanegwad-carmarthen.co.uk** to find details of trade directories, people
from the past, street names, church histories and memorials. Old photographs of Llanfairdfechan are available to view at **www.llanfairfechan.
org.uk**, as well as a community discussion forum and old photos,
whilst articles on many aspects of the history and archaeology of
Abergwyngregyn, including historic pictures, are online at **www.
abergwyngregyn.co.uk**. For the history of Penmaenmawr, including
information on its war memorials and village names, go to **www.
penmaenmawr.com**.
The history of lead and gold mining in the county is explored
at **http://people.exeter.ac.uk/pfclaugh/mhinf/contents.htm#wales**. For
information on Carmarthenshire's part in the nineteenth century
Rebecca Riots, visit the Bro Beca project at **www.brobeca.co.uk/home.
html**.

Denbighshire
Denbighshire Record Office has several indexes at **www.denbighshire.
gov.uk/en-gb/DNAP-6ZQKTQ** for newspapers, personal names, places
and subjects in its archive holdings. The Wrexham Archives and Local

Studies Service pages at **www.wrexham.gov.uk/english/heritage/ archives/index.htm** include a catalogue and downloadable guides of resources, with lists of parish register transcriptions and newspapers, as well as local indexes for statutory birth, marriages and deaths (1837–1950, up to 1997 for births). Similar entries for statutory records in the rest of the county are included on the North Wales BMD site (**www. northwalesbmd.org.uk**).

Clwyd Family History Society (**www.clwydfhs.org.uk**) has photos online from every church in the county, as well as a list of published monumental inscriptions for sale. Extracts from various directories and reference books are included at **www.namesfromclwyd.org.uk**, as well as a master index of names from the printed *Parish Registers of Clwyd*, as transcribed by volunteer members of the society.

The 1871 census for Garthgarmon is online at **http://tinyurl.com/ ydmez8f**. Details of listed buildings in Rosselt are available at **www. rossett.org.uk**, and several resources for the village of Bwlchgwyn, including a gallery of old photos, can be consulted at **www.belton.me. uk**. The website for Llangollen Museum at **www.llangollenmuseum. org.uk** has an online catalogue of useful research sources for the local area, whilst the history of Chirk is briefly explored at **www.chirk.com**. Further links to various websites on neighbouring towns can also be found at the bottom of the page.

Flintshire

Local statutory records indexes for births, marriages and deaths for Flintshire are available at **www.northwalesbmd.org.uk**. The county record site at **http://tinyurl.com/ygfgkbc** has an online record gallery and family history guide, as well as various catalogues and indexes, including databases for parish-based photographic holdings, industrial records, bishops' transcripts, newspapers, and more.

As part of modern Clwyd, records for the county can also be found at **www.namesfromclwyd.org.uk**, and in the holdings of Clwyd Family History Society (see above). A brief history of the county is available at **www.flintshire.org**, whilst a study of seventeenth-century witchcraft in the county is online at the National Library of Wales website (**www. llgc.org.uk/index.php?id=witchcraftcourtofgrearsessi**).

Various resources for Flint, including Roman Catholic registers, directories, burgess lists and books, can be found at **www.cefnpennar.com/ flint/index.htm**. A history of Llanasa is at **http://llanasaconservation**

socie.homestead.com, including old images, whilst a detailed history of Shotton with essays on the ships of John Summers, the railway, the Wepre Hall estate and more, can be consulted at **www.angelfire.com/fl/ shotton**.

The Buckley Society (**www.buckleysociety.org.uk**) has historic photos online, as well as subject and articles indexes as featured in its journal, whilst the Bagillt Heritage Society reveals its local history at **www. bagillt.org.uk**, with various essays on topics of local interest.

Glamorgan

The Glamorgan GENUKI pages are some of the most detailed of the whole project, including various resources, and are most definitely a useful first port of call.

The Glamorgan Archives pages at **www.glamro.gov.uk** include parish registers listings (established and nonconformist), and on online exhibition entitled *Cardiff: the Building of a Capital*. The archive also provides a guide to municipal cemeteries in the county, which can be read at **www.glamro.gov.uk/adobe/municipal.pdf**. The West Glamorgan Archive Service (**www.swansea.gov.uk/westglamorganarchives**) has online exhibitions on *Guildhall Swansea 1934–2009* and the 40th anniversary of Swansea's existence as a city. There are further guides concerning records in its collection such as maritime and political papers, an index of place names, and a gazetteer of localities in West Glamorgan.

Robert Sanders' superb *Wales, England and Maritime Family History Research* pages at **www.glamorganfamilyhistory.co.uk** are absolutely packed with resources on Cardiff and Glamorgan, including essays on various topics of local interest, such as the history of Chartism, the Rebecca Riots, the Merthyr Uprising, the Glamorgan Militia, the history of non-conformism and Methodism in the county, a Cardiff chronology, and much more.

The Glamorgan Family History Society website at **www.rootsweb. ancestry.com/~wlsglfhs** hosts Swansea and Neath militia lists and an article on the parish church at Llandeilo Tal-y-bont, as well as a members only chat forum. Swansea Council (**www.swansea.gov.uk/index.cfm? articleid=467**) has an index for the *Cambrian* newspaper from 1804–1930, as well as lists of newspapers, trade directories and electoral registers available for consultation. On the heritage front, an interactive map with links to historic images from across Swansea, as well as pages on various subjects of local historic interest, are available at **www.**

swanseaheritage.net. For a history of mariners and ships from the city, visit **www.swanseamariners.org.uk**. A list of Cardiff places of worship in existence in 2005 is listed in *Cardiff Places of Worship Survey* at **http://freepages.genealogy.rootsweb.ancestry.com/~cdfplacesofworship**.

The Internet Archive has the parish registers of Llantrithyd (christenings 1597–1810, burials 1571–1810 and marriages 1571–1752) at **www.archive.org/details/registersofllant00llan**, whilst the history of Llangynwyd Parish is at **www.archive.org/details/historyllangynw00 evangoog**. The Explore Gower site at **www.explore-gower.co.uk** has images of several churches and other heritage sites on the peninsula, whilst monumental inscriptions for Cyncoed Church and the war memorial are available on the OGRE site at **www.cefnpennar.com**, as well as a list of landowners from 1873 for the county. Ogmore Valley Local History and Heritage Society's site (**www.ovlhs.btik.com/home. ikml**) has a miners' deaths index (1865–1984), and a digital archive featuring historic photos and documents. A site dedicated to Whitchurch and Llandaff North is available at **www.whitchurchandllandaff.co.uk** containing newspaper clippings and other resources. For genealogical resources for Cymgors, Gwauncaegurwen, the parish of Llangiwg and the Amman Valley, visit **www.tytwp.plus.com/Waun/Waun.html# Contents**.

A history of the Rhondda Valleys is located at **www.anglesey.info/ Rhondda_History.htm** including many photos of old coal mines from the region. The Rhondda Blue Plaque Scheme at **http://tinyurl.com/ yhoqq36** has short biographies on those commemorated, whilst at **www.treorchy.net** you can access an index to papers from the former legal practise of Treharne and Treharne based in Pentre, and now held at Glamorgan Record Office. The *Pillars of Faith* site at **www.pillars-of-faith.com** commemorates the history of the Rhondda's nonconformism.

For the war diaries of the Seventeenth (Service) Battalion of the Welsh regiment (the 'First Glamorgan Bantams') visit **www.seventeenthwelsh. ukf.net**.

Merionethshire

Now mainly in Gwynedd, local statutory records indexes for post-1837 births, marriages and deaths for historic Merionethshire can be found at North Wales BMD (**www.northwalesbmd.org.uk**), whilst the online catalogue for Gwynedd Archives is at **www.gwynedd.gov.uk/gwy_doc. asp?cat=3693&doc=12971&Language=1**. A parish map for the county is available at Gwynedd Family History Society's site at **www.gwynedd fhs.org**.

Part of Merionethshire is also now included with Clwyd, and Clwyd Family History Society has photos from every church from the relevant part of the county at **www.clwydfhs.org.uk/churches/index.html**, with some parish register entries also included in its index at **www.names fromclwyd.org.uk**.

Census resources for Dolgellau, Llanelltyd, Llanfachreth, Barmouth and Dinas Mawddwy, and links to additional resources for other villages including Trawsfynydd, Maentwrog and Llandanwg can be consulted at **http://freepages.history.rootsweb.ancestry.com/~alwyn/D/Census/ index.htm**.

For the history of manganese mining in the county, visit **www. hendrecoed.org.uk/Merioneth-Manganese**.

Monmouthshire
The 1901 Kelly's Directory for Monmouthshire has been completely tran-scribed and is available at **http://freepages.genealogy.rootsweb.ancestry. com/~familyalbum**, providing a useful description of the county and its residents at that point. The *Online Genealogy Resources* website (known as OGRE) is another useful resource, packed with material for the county. Located at **www.cefnpennar.com**, it includes Llanbadog parish registers (1582–1709), a register from Peterson-Super-Ely (1749–1812), monumental inscriptions from several parishes with headstone photos, directory entries and more. The *Forest of Dean Parish Records Project* at **www.forest-of-dean.net** also includes several Monmouth-shire parish records, as well as a wills index for probate at Gloucester (1858–1910).

The Monmouthshire Family History pages at **http://freepages. genealogy.rootsweb.ancestry.com/~monfamilies/monfh.htm** host a detailed parish guide and map, as well as many records for the county, including Catholic Mission and poor law records, parish registers and wills. An equally useful resource is the *1841 Census for Monmouthshire* site (**www.charsbrokenbranches.com/Monmouthshire-files.html**), which amongst its transcriptions hosts parish records for Trelleck, Llandogo, Cymyoy and Lanthony. The *Monmouthshire Marriages* site at **http://free pages.genealogy.rootsweb.ancestry.com/~monfamilies/Monmarrindex. html** has about forty per cent of all marriages in the county indexed from 1725–1812.

For the history of Caerleon visit **www.caerleon.net**, where you will find directories, census transcriptions, an 1840 parish tithe survey and map, parish records and historic photos. Several local history resources for Crosskeys, including a timeline and Kelly's Directory entries from 1914 can be found at **www.crosskeys.me.uk**. The history of Tredegar is at **http://web.ukonline.co.uk/b.gardner/tredegar/tredpage.html**, and as well as copies of the 1881 census, it discusses various topics including links to the American mining town of Scranton, Pennsylvania.

A site for Abertillery at **www.abertillery.net** includes an old tithe map from 1840, as well as an interesting *Tillery Tales* section discussing various subjects such as World War 1 Heroes; there is also a family history section and old photographic images. For the history of the mining village of Cymtillery, with a chronology and information about Cymtillery Colliery, visit **www.cwmtillery.com**.

Montgomeryshire

Now part of Powys, the county archive for Montgomeryshire is included at **www.powys.gov.uk/index.php?id=647&L=0&** (the Powys County Archive Office site), which has a library catalogue and a detailed guide of holdings via the link to its Local Studies Sources section. The *Powys Heritage Online* site at **http://history.powys.org.uk** has several resources for the county, including dedicated sections on Machynlleth and the Dovey Valley, and the district of Llandiloes, with directories listings and other materials.

Montgomeryshire Family History Society has placed many useful resources online at **http://home.freeuk.net/montgensoc**. These include a parish map, pictures of churches from many denominations, views of Old Montgomeryshire, a guide to the use of the Welsh language in the county, and hearth tax returns from 1664–65 for the county's seven hundreds of Cawrse, Cyfeiliog, Deuddwr, Llanfyllin, Llanidloes, Mathrafal, Montgomery, Newtown and Poole. For local statutory indexes compiled post-1837 to births, marriages and deaths, visit **www.northwalesbmd.org.uk**.

A website on the history of Machynlleth and the Dyfi Valley can be found at **http://website.lineone.net/~rkwilli** which includes old photos, tithe maps and more.

Pembrokeshire

CenQuest (**www.cenquest.co.uk**) has several Pembrokeshire censuses (with images for 1871), as well as the 1670 Pembrokeshire hearth tax,

Pembrokeshire-based census records can be accessed through Cenquest. Courtesy Cenquest

St David's Cathedral Monumental inscriptions, and information from the auction of the Orielton Estate in 1856. The indexes are free to consult, but the full entries require a £10 fee for three months access.

Graham Davies' *Pembrokeshire Roots* site at **http://members.lycos.co. uk/Graham_Davies** includes a detailed parish guide (grouped together in the former hundreds of Castlemartin, Cemaes, Cilgerran, Dewisland, Dungleddy, Narberth and Rhos), the *Railways of Pembrokeshire* site, and various links to other sites with Pembrokeshire resources (though some are now broken). As part of Dyfed, further resources can also be found on the Dyfed FHS site at **www.dyfedfhs.org.uk** (see Cardiganshire).

A history and list of mines in Pembrokeshire (also Carmarthenshire and Cardiganshire) can be explored at **http://people.exeter.ac.uk/ pfclaugh/mhinf/pembs1.htm**, whilst the story of the nineteenth century Rebecca Riots can be read at the Bro Beca project site (**www.brobeca. co.uk/home.html**).

For Pembroke's history visit **www.pembrokestory.org.uk**, whilst Tenby's past can be examined at **www.tenbymuseum.org.uk**, where amongst its holdings is a page on Robert Recorde, the inventor of the equals sign! Parish birth, marriage and death indexes are online for Stackpole Elidor, St. Petrox, Bosherton and St Twynnells at **http:// members.lycos.co.uk/John_Richards/register.htm**, whilst a history of Lamphey and Hodgeston is at **www.lamphey.org.uk/sparc/sparc%20 leaflet.html**.

Radnorshire

The historic county of Radnorshire now forms part of Powys, and as such its archival holdings are dealt with in the same Powys repositories as listed for Breconshire, including the Powys County Archive Office (see p. 124). The Powys Digital History Project hosts detailed studies on two communities, entitled *Rhayader and the Elan Valley* and *Presteigne and the Marches*, available at **http://history.powys.org.uk**. A name index to Powys Family History Society's journal *Cronicl Powys* (for the first thirty issues) is at **www.rootsweb.ancestry.com/~wlspfhs/Pages/intro. htm**, whilst articles in the Radnor Society's journal, *Transactions*, are listed at **www.radnorshiresociety.org.uk**.

The *Radnorshire Churches Survey* at **www.cpat.demon.co.uk/projects/ longer/churches/radnor/idxradn.htm** provides details on all churches recorded in the project in 1995–96, which was carried out by the Clwyd-Powys Archaeological Trust.

For a history of Llandrindod, including a guided walk through the town, visit **www.llandrindod.co.uk/HTML/History.htm**.

Chapter Six

SCOTLAND

Scottish resources are mainly in English, but you may find some records also written in either Scots or Gaelic (Gàidhlig). The Scots language is a variant form of the Germanic-based language that became English south of the border. A term which once perplexed me for several weeks from Perth was the constant reference in old weavers' records to the payment of money for a 'football'. This turned out not to in fact refer to the sport of football, but to the payment of a monetary sum known as a 'football' to the trade incorporation, which went into a pot from which dependants could draw support in times of need! Many Scots words can be deciphered via **www.scots-online.org**, whilst to understand older forms of Scottish handwriting visit **www.scottish handwriting.com**.

The following websites on a county by county basis may assist with your research.

Aberdeenshire
The Aberdeen and North East Scotland Family History Society website (**http://anesfhs.org.uk**) hosts a monumental inscription index of 125,000 names from both published and unpublished sources (also covering Banffshire, Kincardineshire and Morayshire), a map of burial grounds in the Scottish north east, kirkyard photos, Aberdeenshire parish details and downloadable family history charts. The Family History Society of Buchan's site (**www.fhsb.org.uk**) also has a map and description of parishes for its area, articles, contact details for local registrars and a downloadable society newsletter, *Aa the Claik*.

A parish map for Aberdeenshire is also available at **www.monikie.org. uk/parishmap.jpg**, whilst Colin Milne's excellent North East Scotland site (**http://myweb.tiscali.co.uk/nescotland**) includes militia records, newspaper extracts, graves photos, old school photos and more.

For Aberdeen, an 1895 parish map is available at **http://tinyurl.com/ yjjrw9g**, whilst Tim Lambert's history of the city is at **www.local histories.org/aberdeen.html**. *The Armorial Ensigns of the Royal Burgh of Aberdeen*, written by John Cruickshank in 1888, has been republished by the Internet Archive at **www.archive.org/details/armorialensignso 00crui**. Burial records for Aberdeen are on Deceased Online.

The Electric Scotland website at **www.electricscotland.com/history/ guilds** hosts a transcript of the 1887 book *A History of the Aberdeen Incorporated Trades* by Ebenezer Bain, whilst the *Aberdeen Built Ships Project* at **www.aberdeenships.com** includes a database and history of some local shipbuilders. For the history of Grampian Police Force visit **www.grampian.police.uk/About.aspx?id=22&pid=30;31;2**.

The University of Aberdeen's Manuscript and Archive Collections catalogue can be searched at **www.abdn.ac.uk/historic/Manuscripts. shtml**. The university is also responsible for the Scottish Emigration Database at **www.abdn.ac.uk/emigration**, which lists some 21,000 passengers who sailed from Glasgow and Greenock, though is contained to voyages between January 1st and April 30 1923.

Resources for the history of families and communities in Glenbuchat can be found at **http://genepool.bio.ed.ac.uk/Glenbuchat/peopleand places.html**. Daviot village's history is at **www.daviot.org**, with holdings including the school register from 1874–1923. The village of Birse is covered at **http://birsefolk.id.au** and includes censuses, strays, baptisms (1761–1779 and 1820–21) and marriages (1782–1799 and 1820–1826). A Register of Baptisms from 1763–1801 at Bairnie and Tillydesk can be examined on the Internet Archive at **www.archive.org/stream/scottish recordso19scotuoft#page/n1/mode/2up**. Census material for Kinnethmont is available at **www.kinnethmont.co.uk**, as are old school photos and war memorial transcriptions.

Records for Upper and Lower Cabrach are available at **www.three stones.co.uk** and include war memorials, local songs, local books and more, whilst the *Genealogy of the Cabrach* site at **http://myweb.tiscali. co.uk/stuartpetrie** has records from various sources including censuses. Vital records for Strathdon are freely available at **http://sites.google. com/site/strathdonvitals**. For the history of the Howe, visit **www. mearns.org/history.htm** to find descriptions of several villages.

Angus
Previously known as Forfarshire until 1928, the history of Angus is dominated by the city of Dundee. Historic maps of Dundee, Forfarshire and the Firth of Tay are available at **http://tinyurl.com/yjtdxsy**, whilst a maritime history of Tayside, including trade maps, essays on the flax industry, a mariners' database and more is available at **www.dmcsoft. com/tamh**. A list of some of the more prominent places and people from the area, as well as pages on the Tay Bridge Disaster of 1879, the Black Watch Museum and the Forfar Witches can be viewed at **www.tayroots. com/HistoryofAngusandDundee/Local-History.asp**, whilst a history of the county's police force is at **www.tayside.police.uk/history.php**.

The county archive site (**www.angus.gov.uk/history/archives**) includes several online photo collections, as well as an *Angus People Index* and an *Angus Building Image Index* relating to its holdings. Dundee has its own archive site at **www.dundeecity.gov.uk/archive** which includes council minutes dating back to 1553. The council also runs a historic images site entitled *Photopolis* at **www.dundeecity.gov.uk/photodb/main.htm**, which has some 5000 old photographs of the city.

Helping the council are the Friends of Dundee City Archives, which has done some excellent work in transcribing many of the archive's holdings and placing them online at **www.fdca.org.uk**. Included are databases such as the 1801 census for Dundee, several burial collections including the Howff Cemetery, and additional resources such as the Lockit Book of Dundee, a nineteenth century database of Dundee ships, poorhouse records for both the city and Liff and Benvie, Wesleyan Chapel records, Cowgate school records (1899–1910), and much more. The Tay Valley Family History Society, based in Dundee, has a searchable library catalogue of its resources online at **www.tayvalleyfhs.org.uk**.

Unlock the Boxes at **http://tinyurl.com/yjbkvgp** carries an interesting virtual exhibition on eighteenth century life in Angus, whilst the Lamb Collection, available at **http://sites.scran.ac.uk/lamb** has essays on subjects such as entertainment, cholera and crime and punishment, as derived from research into the collection compiled by Alexander Crawford Lamb (1843–97).

Various resources for Monikie and surrounding areas are available at **www.monikie.org.uk**, including maps and hearth tax returns. Burials for Barry (1746–1800) are recorded at **http://tinyurl.com/ygwdr8q**, whilst the Internet Archive has a reproduction of an 1895 book entitled *The Parish of Longforgan; a Sketch of its Church and People* available at **www.archive.org/details/parishoflongforg00philiala**.

Argyll

Argyll Archives, based in Lochgilphead, has provided online guides to its resources at **www.argyll-bute.gov.uk/content/atoz/services/archives**, whilst a Local Studies Department guide to the council's holdings at Dunoon, including a list of newspapers held there, is at **http://tinyurl. com/yzywb2q**.

The Lochaber And North Argyll Family History Group (**www. lochaberandnorthargyllfamilyhistorygroup.org.uk**) has parish maps for Argyll and detailed church denomination guides for the region, as well as a listing of society resources. Highland Family History Society's site (**www.highlandfhs.org.uk**) also covers Argyll, providing a publications list, and several indexes for gravestones, articles, the 1851 census and names featured in family trees held by the society.

The censuses from 1841–71 for Kilbrandon and Kilchattan parish are available at **http://genealogy4you.com/hobbyco**, whilst a 1779 census of the Duke of Argyll's estates can be accessed at **http://web.ncf.ca/cv297/ app1779.html**. The Ralston genealogy site at **www.ralston genealogy. com** includes monumental inscriptions for some Kintyre-based cemeteries, as well as other local resources. A brief outline of the history of Appin can be read at **www.appinhistoricalsociety.co.uk**, whilst a discussion forum for those with family from Ardchattan (Barcaldine, Benderloch, N. Connel and Bonawe) is at **www.benderloch.org.uk/ forum**.

Records for Skipness parish, in the form of rent books, parish records, censuses, kirk session minutes, map and folklore are available at **www. rootsweb.ancestry.com/~sctcskip**. For resources covering Knapdale, visit **www.knapdalepeople.com**. Finally if your ancestor was of the law breaking kind, visit the Inveraray Jail site at **www.inverarayjail.co.uk** to look-up the facility's prison records database.

Ayrshire

Ayrshire Roots (**www.ayrshireroots.com**) is essentially an online parish clerk site, packed with resources including parish records, gazetteer descriptions and more. Ayrshire History (**www.ayrshirehistory.org.uk**) contains many fascinating articles on the county's history, whilst historic photos from the county are available at **http://homepages. rootsweb.ancestry.com/~ayrshire**. A subscription-based site at **www. ayrshireancestors.co.uk** has several monumental inscriptions.

Ayrshire Archives has some online resources at **www.ayrshirearchives. org.uk** including a virtual exhibition on the history of Afro-Caribbean people linked to the county in the eighteenth and nineteenth centuries, as well as searchable databases for burgesses and guild brethren for Irvine (1715–1920) and an *Irvine Harbour Trust Harbour Book Cargoes In and Out* database (1821–24).

Historic maps for Ayrshire can be found at **http://tinyurl.com/yfenvfo**, and an 1819 map of Kilmarnock at **www.dangly.com/kilmarnock/maps/Kilmarnock%202.jpg**.

For North Ayrshire, the *Three Towners* site at **www.threetowners.com** has material for Ardossan, Saltcoats and Stevenston, including the 1819, 1822 and 1836 censuses, headstones information, newspaper intimations and poor relief database. The *North Ayrshire Remembers* site at **http://northayrshireremembers.tripod.com** includes information on those from Largs who fell during the two world wars, as well as a partial index of nineteenth century listings for Largs people noted in the *Glasgow Herald* in the nineteenth century. The site also has some links to resources for West Kilbride and Cumbrae. A history of Skelmorlie and Wemyss Bay is available at **www.scribd.com/doc/1289541/Skelmorlie-Original-Walter-Smart-History-1968**.

Monumental inscriptions and OPR material for Dalrymple can be found at **www.geographyhigh.connectfree.co.uk/dalrymple.html**, whilst the parish church page for Ochiltree at **http://ochiltreechurch.homestead.com** includes a headstone index. The Maybole community website (**www.maybole.org**) has the local 1841 census, with hearth tax rolls from 1691 for the whole county also available at **www.maybole.org/history/Archives/hearthtax1691.htm**. A baptismal register for Stair (1862–1917) can be consulted at **http://stairchurch.homestead.com**.

Of the four family history societies in the county, the best online resources can be found at East Ayrshire's site (**www.eastayrshirefhs.org.uk**), which has a map of the area, a forum (members only), a parish list and names of towns and villages, whilst Troon@Ayrshire's site (**www.troonayrshirefhs.org.uk**) provides transcriptions from registers of applications for poor relief in Dreghorn parish (1872–1890), an Ayrshire parish list, and an article on the Hammermen of Irvine.

Banffshire
The Moray Burial Ground Research Group site at **www.mbgrg.org** includes details for some headstones found within cemeteries in Banffshire (see Morayshire). Inscriptions for the parish of Bortiphnie can be found at **www.botriphnie.org.uk/Parish.htm**, along with further

resources for both it and the estate of Drummuir, such as lists of kirk ministers from 1574. Further resources are available at the Aberdeen and North East Scotland Family History Society site (see p. 135)

An interesting paper on the use of aliases and patronymics in Upper Banffshire, by Stuart Mitchell, is available at **http://tinyurl.com/o947jo**, which quotes many church records as part of its source material, naming many individuals.

Berwickshire

Borders Family History Society has an interactive parish map at **www. bordersfhs.org.uk/b_shire.asp** with detailed guides to records held by both it and other repositories in Scotland. Census records from 1841–1861 have been made freely available at **www.maxwellancestry.com**, with many returns linked to maps at the National Library of Scotland, as well as confirmed inter-census links to show family progressions across time. A list of heritage site locations in the county can be found at **www.scottishbordersheritage.co.uk/49842**.

Maxwell Ancestry provides many free to access databases for the Borders counties

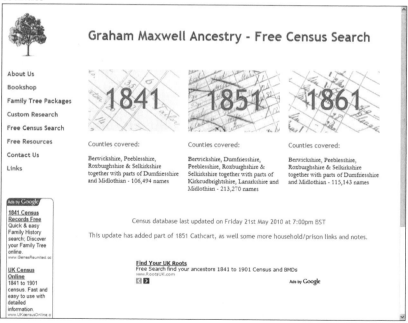

An index to Berwickshire graveyard locations is online at **www.roots web.ancestry.com/~sctbew/Cemeteries/cemindex.htm**. Some Berwickshire death records from 1855–1881, marriages from 1865, and births from 1866–67 are freely available at **http://freepages.genealogy.rootsweb. ancestry.com/~connochie/bdm**, whilst a one place study for Whitsome at **http://homepages.ipact.nl/~robertson** has gravestone inscriptions, school records and the 1841 census for the parish. Monumental inscription from Eyemouth Cemetery and Eyemouth Old Kirk are indexed at **www.memento-mori.co.uk**. The kirk session book for Bunkle and Preston from 1665–1690 is available from the Internet Archive at **www.archive.org/details/sessionbookbunk00clubgoog**.

The *Old Scottish Borders Photo Archive* site at **www.ettrickgraphics. com/bordersindex.htm** has many images from Berwickshire, whilst photos for Eyemouth, Cockburnspath and Cove can also be found on-line at **www.fairbairnfamily.webeden.co.uk**, along with some limited census returns.

Bute

The former county of Buteshire consisted of more than just the island of Bute, with part of the mainland to its north included as well as the two Cumbrae islands and Arran.

A general history of the island of Bute is available at **www.isle-of-bute. com/about-bute**. A more comprehensive site is Bute Sons and Daughters Through the Centuries (**www.butesonsanddaughters.co.uk**) which includes a surname index of those recorded in the 1841 census, as well as some film records of Bute, a history of Rothesay pier and more. For the 1841 census for Cumbrae, Kilbride, Kilmory and Kingarth visit **http://freepages.genealogy.rootsweb.ancestry.com/~relys4u**.

Various BMDs being researched by those with Buteshire links and some monumental inscriptions can also be found at **http://members. shaw.ca/Buteshire**.

Caithness

Whilst Caithness is included within the coverage of the Highland Family History Society (see Invernessshire), it also has its own dedicated society, the website of which (**www.caithnessfhs.org.uk**) contains a list of contents from past journals, a beginners' page and publications list. There is also a genealogical discussion forum for the county at **http:// forum.caithness.org/forumdisplay.php?f=9**. For a parish map, visit **www.oddquine.co.uk/Genealogy/index.html**.

The Highland Archives site at **www.iprom.co.uk/archives** has many resources, particularly on the local and military history of the county, including WW1 rolls of honour. The *Caithness War Memorials* site at **www.caithness.org/atoz/warmemorials/index.htm** also pays tribute to fallen sons of Caithness from across the county.

For people with ancestry from the Threipland estates in Caithness, it is also worth consulting the Thriepland database hosted by Perth and Kinross Archives, which lists many tenants there (see p. 155).

The 1841 census for Bower, Canisbay, Dunnet and Halkirk is online at **http://freepages.genealogy.rootsweb.ancestry.com/~relys4u**, whilst the parish register of Canisbay from 1652–1666 can be consulted on the Internet Archive at **www.archive.org/details/parishregisterso67cani**.

Clackmannanshire

The smallest county with the longest name! Stobie's 1783 map of Clackmannanshire can be found at **www.chalmers-family.org/genuki/ CLK/map.jpg**. The same map, along with maps of Westfield from 1845, 1848 and 1898 can be found at **http://freepages.genealogy.rootsweb. ancestry.com/~russellsofwestfield**. Census transcriptions for Westfield can also be browsed at the site.

For a summary of the holdings of Clackmannanshire Archives visit **www.clacksweb.org.uk/culture/archives/**. Central Scotland Family History Society lists members' interests for the county on its site at **www.csfhs.org.uk**.

Memento Mori (**www.memento-mori.co.uk**) hosts an index to monumental inscriptions for both Alva and Tillicoultry. For inscriptions in Tullibody visit **http://jimpson.freewebsites.com/AuldKirk/AuldKirk. html**. The site also contains a page on *Stories about the Auld Kirk*.

A history of Menstrie Castle is available at **www.menstriecastle.co. uk/index.htm**, along with some photos.

Dumfriesshire

The Friends of the Archives of Dumfries and Galloway site at **www.dgcommunity.net/historicalindexes** has many transcriptions of Dumfriesshire-based records, including census returns, kirk session minutes, jail books and bail bond registers, Dean of Guild plans, shipping registers and Poor Board minutes. The Dumfriesshire and Galloway Natural History and Antiquarian Society site (**www.dgnhas. org.uk**) hosts an index to its *Transactions* periodical (1862–2008). The

Scottish Page at **http://homepages.rootsweb.ancestry.com/~scottish** has links to many resources for the county as well as details of others with research interests there.

For images of Dumfriesshire churches and graveyards visit **http:// homepages.rootsweb.ancestry.com/~dfsgal**, whilst monumental inscriptions for many graveyards in the county can be found at **www.john macmillan.co.uk/indx_cemetery.html**.

Maxwell Ancestry has some handy resources at **www.maxwell ancestry.com** for the county, the most important of which are valuation rolls for Annan, Applegarth, Caerlaverock, Canonbie, Closeburn, Cummertrees, Dalton and Dornock from 1896–97. The site also provides free census records transcriptions from 1841–1861.

For irregular marriages carried out at Gretna, an index from 1795–1895 is available at **www.achievements.co.uk/services/gretna/index. php**, though the records have also been digitised and made available at Ancestry. Also for Gretna, the Devil's Porridge website (**www.devils porridge.co.uk**) deals with the history of munitions manufacturing at HM Factory Gretna in the twentieth century.

Memorials for Sanquhar Kirkyard can be consulted at **http://freepages. history.rootsweb.ancestry.com/~cdobie/Sanquhar.htm**. A history of the parish of Glencairn is at **www.archive.org/details/parishglencairn00 montgoog**, and the history of the royal burgh of Annan at **www.annan. org.uk/history/index.html**. A list of Provosts in Dumfries is at **http:// homepages.rootsweb.ancestry.com/~scottish/Provosts.html**.

If your ancestors migrated overseas, a list of many born in the county who died in Canada is available at **http://homepages.rootsweb.ancestry. com/~scottish/D-GForeignBuried.html**.

Dunbartonshire

The comprehensive *Vale of Leven Story* (**www.valeofleven.org.uk**) contains detailed histories of towns and villages in West Dunbartonshire, as well as a discussion board and essays on various aspects of local history. Old photos of Balloch, and a transcription of the 1881 census for the village, are available at **www.visit-balloch.com**.

For Dumbarton, the *More Than a Memory* oral history project (**www.melvich.pwp.blueyonder.co.uk/mtam.htm**) has many recorded extracts in a dedicated multimedia section, as well as historic photos from the town – a highlight is cine film of the VE Day celebrations from 1945. An online exhibition of the Clydebank Blitz is located at **www.**

glasgow.gov.uk/en/Residents/Libraries/Collections/Blitz, and a list of civilian war dead from Clydebank at **http://thor.prohosting.com/ ~hughw/wardead1.txt**, for surnames beginning with A and B. For later surnames in the alphabet, replace *wardead1* with *wardead2, wardead3* etc. in the website address.

Memento Mori at **www.memento-mori.co.uk** has monumental inscriptions for Auld Isle (Kirkintilloch), Cadder, Campsie (cemetery and churchyard) and Kilsyth (cemetery and churchyard). Inscriptions for Rosneath, with a churchyard plan, can be viewed at **http://members. madasafish.com/~fairenough**.

East Lothian (Haddingtonshire until 1921)

Until 1921, East Lothian was known as Haddingtonshire, with Haddington the county town. The Lothians Family History Society covers the area, and its website (**www.lothiansfhs.org.uk**) has a map and a discussion forum. For information on friendly societies, incorporations, guilds and ancient orders in the county visit **www.historyshelf.org/ shelf/friend/index.php**.

A graveyard index for St. Mary's Church in Haddington is on the church's website at **www.stmaryskirk.com/index.htm**, whilst burial ground surveys for the parish of Traprain are at **www.ejclark.force9. co.uk**, with records for Prestonkirk, Stenton and Whittingehame.

For Bolton and Saltoun, parish records from 1998 onwards and burial records are hosted at **http://ndhm.org.uk**. The Dunbar and District History Society site (**www.djma.org.uk/dunbar/ddhs**) has many old photos online for its area.

Fife

Fife's family history society website is one of the best in Scotland. Located at **www.fifefhs.org** it provides many free resources, with at the time of writing some 89 separate databases, ranging from Fife Sheriff Court deeds (1715–1809) to Dunfermline Weavers freemen entry books (1596–1863). There are also directory records, militia accounts, dissenting church records, pre-1855 death records and more.

The Fife Council Archives site (**http://tinyurl.com/ygnwfem**) includes a searchable catalogue and databases such as *Escaped Prisoners and Patients in 1942* and an *Index to Register of Photographs of Criminals 1912–23*. The University of St Andrew's Special Collections Department (**www.st-andrews.ac.uk/specialcollections**) has details on its various collections, and links to sub sites such as the *Library Photographic Archive* at **http://special.st-andrews.ac.uk/saspecial**, and its own genealogical holdings.

For biographical information on the great and the good, the Internet Archive hosts the *Biographical Dictionary of Eminent Men of Fife* (1866) at **www.archive.org/details/biographicaldic00conogoog** and *Lives of Eminent Men* (1846) at **www.archive.org/details/liveseminentmen00 brucgoog**.

A generic Fife site at **www.thefifepost.com** has many interesting sections on subjects such as the county's burghs, witches and trials, providing an interesting overview. A name index for Fife newspapers (1833–1987) held at Cupar Library is online at Ancestry.

The parish registers of Dunfermline (1561–1700) can be consulted at **www.archive.org/details/scottishrecordso32scotuoft**, whilst Scots Find (**www.scotsfind.org**) hosts the *Presbytery Book of Kirkcaldy* and the *Local Records of Dysart*. Directories, voters rolls, censuses, hearth tax records and more for Newport, Wormit, and Forgan are available at **www. twentytwoflassroad.co.uk**, whilst the Scoonie 1841 census is online at **http://member.melbpc.org.au/~andes/scoonie.html**.

The history of the royal burgh of Burntisland is outlined at **www. burntisland.net** and includes the town's charter from 1541. A general history of Kincardine on Forth is recorded at **www.rocinante.demon. co.uk/klhg/klhgindx.htm**, whilst the history of Kingsbarns is further outlined at **www.kingsbarnslinks.com/villguide/history.htm**.

The county's mining history is dealt with at **www.users.zetnet.co.uk/ mmartin/fifepits**, which also includes the *Kingdom of Fife Mining Industry Memorial Book* database.

Invernessshire

Probably the most comprehensive site for Invernessshire is the *Am Baile* website at **www.ambaile.org.uk** (Gaelic for 'The Village'), which covers much of the Highlands. It hosts various materials, both indexed and digitised, including newspaper indexes, maps, plans, photos, books and Gaelic resources, all for free.

The Old Home Town Image Archive (**www.theoldhometown. com**) includes historic images of Inverness, whilst the Scottish Highlander Photo Archive at **www.scottishhighlanderphotoarchive.co.uk/ genealogists.html** will host some 20,000 historic black and white photos

The Gateway to the Scottish Highlands – the impressive Am Baile project.
Courtesy of Am Baile/Highland Libraries

of individuals when completed, a great proportion of which come from Invernessshire.

Highland Family History Society covers the county, and its site at **www.highlandfhs.org.uk** includes an index for gravestones, a list of articles in the society's publications, members' interests, an 1851 census index and a further list of names found in compiled family trees submitted to the society.

A database of some pre-1850 Invernessshire vital records can be consulted at **http://freepages.genealogy.rootsweb.ancestry.com/~ked1/Glen3.html**. The Scots Find website hosts an *Inverness Register of Testaments* at **www.scotsfind.org/databases_free/freedatabaseindex.htm**.

The Moidart Local History Group (**www.moidart.org.uk/index.htm**) has various resources online for free, such as its Glen Moidart papers (including estate rentals), and some for members only, such as the 1841 census. A history of Ardersier and Petty can be found at **www. btinternet.com/~ardersier/history.htm**.

If your ancestor was from Urquhart, a database of Chelsea Pension records showing soldiers discharged from the British Army who gave

Mrs Serafton and family, 86 Church Street, Inverness. Courtesy of the Scottish Highlander Photo Archive

the parish as their birthplace is at **http://freepages.genealogy.rootsweb. ancestry.com/~ked1/WO97.htm**. If your ancestor emigrated to Australia, the Invernessshire Emigrant Index (**http://freepages.genealogy.rootsweb.ancestry.com/~maddenps/ INVEM1.htm**) lists many of those who sailed to New South Wales and Queensland. Databases of emigrants who sailed with the Highlands and Islands Emigration Society between 1852 and 1857 are also available through the Scottish Archive Network site at **www.scan.org.uk/ researchrtools/emigration.htm** and at **www.angelfire.com/ns/bkeddy/ HIES/1.html**. For the stories of many forcibly evicted in the Highland Clearances, visit **www.theclearances.org**.

Kincardineshire
Images from many of Kincardineshire's churches are available at Colin Milne's NE Scotland site at **http://myweb.tiscali.co.uk/nescotland**. Information from war memorials across the county can be consulted at **www.btinternet.com/~amchardy/WarMemorials.htm**.

The Portal to Portlethen site at **www.old-portlethen.co.uk** has many essays on the history of Portlethen, including subjects as diverse as privates and privateers, tee names, farming, and the church and clergy. For a history of Woodstone Fishing Station visit **www.woodston fishingstation.co.uk/woodston_fishing/history.shtml**.

Some census transcriptions from Garvock, Laurencekirk and Fordoun have been transcribed and made available at **http://tinyurl. com/yzetwsy**.

Kinrossshire
Kinross is today jointly administered with Perth though Perth and Kinross Council. Its archive site at **http://tinyurl.com/ltbvod** has several online databases, mainly for Perthshire, but includes a downloadable Genealogy Index which incorporates names from Kinross.

The 1841 census for Kinross can be consulted at **http://member. melbpc.org.au/~andes/scotland.html**. Kinross vehicle registrations, licenses and owners from 1904–1952 have been transcribed from records held at Dundee Council Archives and made available at **www. fdca.org.uk/FDCATransport1.html**, which includes addresses for all those named.

The Kinross Museum website (**www.kinrossmuseum.co.uk**) has several online exhibitions of interest, including items dedicated to burgh folk and St Serf's Island.

Kirkcudbrightshire
A modern map of Kirkcudbrightshire, along with some local family histories and researchers' interests is available at the Scottish Page at **http://homepages.rootsweb.ancestry.com/~scottish**, whilst free 1851 census transcriptions for part of the county are available at **www. maxwellancestry.com**. A handful of cemetery records from twelve parishes within the county are also online at **www.johnmacmillan. co.uk/indx_cemetery.html**, whilst many more can be found at **www. kirkyards.co.uk** for the parishes of Borgue, Buittle, Colvend and Southwick, Parton, Rerrick, Tongland and Twynholm.

The Old Kircudbright site (**www.old-kirkcudbright.net**) contains a parish and burgh history, as well as valuation rolls, parish records such as OPR deaths from 1826–1853, stent rolls, census records for poorhouses in the county, and more. A history of the parish church is also available at **www.kirkcudbrightparish.org.uk**, though the site hosts no records. For the names of volunteers who joined the Urr Company Stewartry Kircudbright Volunteer Infantry on July 16th 1808, visit **http://donjaggi.net/galloway/urrvolunteers1808.html**.

A town history for Dalbeattie is available at **www.dalbeattie.com/ history**, which includes information on the granite quarries, port and industrial mills in the area. For the parish of Buittle visit **www.buittle. org.uk** to see historic postcards, valuation rolls and OPR records (including some Roman Catholic records from 1704–1811), as well as gazetteer descriptions.

Lanarkshire
The historic county of Lanarkshire is dominated by Glasgow, Scotland's largest city. The Glasgow City Archives website at **www.glasgow.gov. uk/en/Residents/Library_Services/The_Mitchell/Archives** provides a wealth of detail on the institution's holdings, with informative guides on collections related to schools, estates, shipbuilding, poor law material, business, police, sasines, church and more. In addition are links to the *Virtual Mitchell* photographic collection and the *Blitz on Clydeside* exhibition.

The University of Glasgow Archives Services site (**www.gla.ac.uk/ archives**) has links to both the Scottish Business Archive and the University Archive, with searchable catalogues and guides. The university celebrates its own history at **www.universitystory.gla.ac.uk**, which includes a graduate list (1496–1896) and Rolls of Honour.

The Mitchell Library in Glasgow. Author's collection

The *Radical Glasgow* site at **www.gcu.ac.uk/radicalglasgow**, produced by Caledonian University, has various essays on the insurrections, uprisings and protest movements to have sprung up in the past, from the weaver's strike of 1787 to the foundation of the Scottish Labour Party. The history of Glasgow's hammermen, as recorded by the Scottish Records Society in 1912, can be read at **www.archive.org/ details/historyofhammerm00lums**.

The Glasgow Story (**www.theglasgowstory.com**) has various essays on the city's history, and includes digitised copies of the valuation rolls for 1913–1914, as well as electoral ward maps. For reminiscences, mainly from Bridgeton, visit the Glesca Pals site at **www.glesga. ukpals.com**, where you will find old school photos, a forum and more. To the city's west, *Anderston Then and Now* (**www.glesga.ukpals.com/ profiles/anderston.htm**) recalls the parish's history.

A Most Curious Murder (**www.amostcuriousmurder.com**) tells the story of the killing of Madeleine Smith in 1857, a well compiled case study of murder and trial in nineteenth century Scotland. With matters religious, the *Diary of a Church Elder 1853–54* at **www.garrion.co.uk/**

diary1853 provides insights into the city's life by an elder from Hutchesontown United Presbyterian Church.

The city's urban built environment is explored at **www.bestlaid schemes.com**, whilst old streets in Glasgow which changed their names before the 1940s are listed at **www.glasgowguide.co.uk/info-streets changed1.html**.

Many monumental inscriptions for the Glasgow and Lanarkshire can be found at the *Memento Mori* site at **www.memento-mori.co.uk**, whilst a database of interments in the city's Southern Necropolis is available at **www.southernnec.20m.com/index.html**. The *Glasgow Evening Times Roll of Honour* index for the First World War is available in PDF format at **http://tinyurl.com/y88djse**. The city's first trade directory, the 1787 Nathaniel Jones Directory of Glasgow, is online at **www.glasgowstories. com**, whilst a later directory from 1927 can be browsed at **http:// freepages.genealogy.rootsweb.ancestry.com/~glasgow/index-glas.htm**. Glasgow Directories from 1809–10, 1815 and 1818–28 are found on the Internet Archive (**www.archive.org**).

A Register of Testaments for Hamilton and Campsie (1564–1800) is available at **www.scotsfind.org**. The history of the county's mining, ironworks and steel industries can be explored at both **www.sorbie. net/lanarkshire_mining_industry.htm** and **http://myweb.tiscali.co.uk/ steelworks/Steelworks%20index.htm**. For Airdrie's history visit **www. airdrie.net**, whilst names for those lost from the town in the First World War are at **www.freewebs.com/dt1078**. Nearby Monklands is covered at **www.monklands.co.uk/cigp/Irishphil.htm**, which includes a Lanarkshire parish map and resources on Irish migration to Lanarkshire.

A parish list for the county is available at the Glasgow and West of Scotland Family History Society site at **www.gwsfhs.org.uk**, along with the society's library catalogue. The Lanarkshire Family History Society site at **www.lanarkshirefhs.org.uk** also offers an online discussion forum open to the public.

Midlothian (formerly Edinburghshire)
Until 1921 Midlothian was the County of Edinburgh, and as with Glasgow in Lanarkshire, the city dominates the county and its history. A map of the capital's parish boundaries is at **www.hoodfamily.info/ misc/miscedinmaplarge.html**.

The Local History and Heritage department site at **www.edinburgh. gov.uk/internet/leisure/CEC_local_history_and_heritage** provides links to many resources at both Central Library and Edinburgh City Archives, as well as links to projects such as the *Capital Collections* project, depicting people and places from the seventeenth century to the present day. The facility has also placed a *Register of Aliens* in the city from 1798–1825 online at **http://tinyurl.com/yhsq67z**.

The Lothians Family History Society site (**www.lothiansfhs.org.uk**) has a discussion forum, but this does not cover Edinburgh, only the surrounding county (and East and West Lothian).

Scots Find (**www.scotsfind.org**) spoils you for choice with its holdings for Edinburgh and Leith, including transcriptions of apprentice register, burgess rolls, marriages and burials, testaments, processes and decreets, and more. Maxwell Ancestry (**www.maxwellancestry.com**) also has some Midlothian censuses from 1841–1861 and editions of *Chambers Edinburgh Journal* from 1832.

The Internet Archive has many digitised Scottish Record Society publications concerning Edinburgh. A *Register of Burials in the Chapel Royal or Abbey of Holyroodhouse 1706–1900* is at **www.archive.org/details/scottishrecordso14scotuoft**, whilst marriages from 1564–1800 for Holyroodhouse and Canongate are online at **www.archive.org/details/scottishrecordso34scotuoft**. Edinburgh marriages from 1595–1700 are at **www.archive.org/details/registerofmarria33edin**, and from 1701–1750 at **www.archive.org/details/scottishrecordso23scotuoft**. A burial register for the churchyard of Restalrig can also be consulted by visiting **www.archive.org/details/scottishrecordso20scotuoft**.

The Lothian Health Services Archives site at **www.lhsa.lib.ed.ac.uk** has a searchable catalogue of holdings for medical matters, whilst the *Friendly Societies in Edinburgh, the Lothians and Fife* site at **www.historyshelf.org/shelf/friend/index.php** has much on the area's guilds and incorporations. Scotland's most iconic structure, the Forth Bridge, was built at a heavy price, and a database of those who died during its construction is hosted at **www.forthbridgememorial.org**. For the history of coal mining in the county, visit **www.hoodfamily.info/index.html**. If your ancestors were Edinburgh-based photographers, you may find more on them at **www.edinphoto.org.uk**.

Elsewhere, a one place study for Corstorphine at **www.angelfire.com/ct2/corstorphine** has directories and the local 1841 census. A similar study for Duddingston at **www.ancestor.abel.co.uk/Duddingston.html** has poll tax testaments, parish records, monumental inscriptions, and other resources. A history of Currie with war memorial records can be viewed at **www.ma.hw.ac.uk/ccc/history**. A blog-based site on the history of Leith is at **www.leithhistory.co.uk**, with the town also covered at **www.leithlocalhistorysociety.org.uk** through the Leith Local History Society, which provides a useful timeline. A host of useful resources for Granton exists at **www.grantonhistory.org**, and for a pictorial history of Niddrie visit **http://niddrie.tripod.com**.

Moray

The *Local Heritage Services in Moray* website at **http://libindx.moray. gov.uk/mainmenu.asp** includes searchable databases of people, places and subjects contained within the county's archives.

The *Moray Burial Ground Research Group* (**www.mbgrg.org**) carries a headstone index, including forename, surname, age and year of death (where known), and in the case of war memorials, regiment. Burial grounds and memorials can be searched individually, and there is a dedicated index for inscriptions found on buried headstones uncovered by the team during its survey work of old cemeteries in the region – the full transcriptions can be sourced from the society's publications. The website also hosts a gallery, a map of the area, a research progress chart and newsletters.

The *Moray Family History Sharing* site at **www.wakefieldfhs.org.uk/ morayweb/index.htm** has a message board, databases for the 1851 and 1861 censuses, photographs from the county and several further Moray-based resources.

A site for Lossiemouth is found at **www.lossiefowk.co.uk** which contains various records and forums, including details from the war memorials and articles on local subjects such as fishing.

Nairnshire

Nairnshire, to the east of Inverness, is covered by several of the same resources focussing on the Highland capital and the Highlands. The Am Baile website at **www.ambaile.org.uk** (see Invernessshire) has many resources for Nairn-based folk, as does the Scottish Highlander Photo Archive at **www.scottishhighlanderphotoarchive.co.uk/genealogists.html**.

Nairnshire is covered by the Highland Family History Society at **www. highlandfhs.org.uk** (see Invernessshire). A page dedicated to the war memorial in Cawdor is available at **www.spanglefish.com/CWMC**, which includes detailed information on the fallen.

Orkney

Orkney consists of several islands north of Caithness, and was not annexed to the Scottish Crown until 1472, having previously been under Norwegian rule for the previous six centuries.

The Orkney Library and Archive site (**www.orkneylibrary.org.uk**) has an online catalogue of resources held at the facility and some resources which members can access from home. It also hosts collections of photos taken by Tom Kent and William H. Houston, and has its own dedicated and often humorous blog at **http://orkneyarchive.blogspot. com**.

An interactive map at **www.ancestralorkney.com** contains lists of the most common names found on each of the islands, and information on some famous Orcadians. For historic images of the island, almost 8000 photographs are hosted at **www.theoldhometown.com**. Further maps, and gravestones from the islands of Rousay, Egilsay, Wyre and Eynhallow, are available at **www.rousayroots.com**. The site also hosts censuses for these islands from 1841–1901 (with Eynhallow uninhabited since 1851), and various family histories. Records for Orphir, North Ronaldsay and Stromness, including Free Church kirk sessions, can be found at **http://meg-greenwood.110mb.com**.

Orkney Genealogy's site (**www.cursiter.com**) has an impressive index of baptisms, marriages and deaths, some digitised images from *Ane Account of the Ancient & Present State of Orkney* by the minister of Kirkwall in 1684, and links to useful resources elsewhere. For South Ronaldsay and Burray visit **www.southronaldsay.net** for resources including a database of the 1821 census, covering the two islands, Swona and the Pentland Skerries. Various extracts from the 1841 census can be found at **http://tinyurl.com/ycdbnpz**. The Orkney Family History Society site (**www.orkneyfhs.co.uk**) has a searchable name index of the 1841 to 1901 Orkney censuses, though only provides a frequency of returns for non-members.

Peeblesshire

A History of Peeblesshire published in 1925–27 is online at **www.tweedie. org/hist_buc.htm**, a site which also hosts maps and various church and monuments pictures from the county. The 1868 Imperial Gazetteer of Scotland's description of Peeblesshire can also be consulted at **www. rootsweb.ancestry.com/~sctpee/genuki/peeblesshire.htm**.

Borders Family History Society has a page dedicated to Peeblesshire at **www.bordersfhs.org.uk/p_shire.asp**, containing an interactive parish map with links to pages containing information on various records held within the society's archive and elsewhere across Scotland.

The 1841–1861 censuses from Peeblesshire have been transcribed and made freely available at **www.maxwellancestry.com**. As with its other borders counties holdings, the locations in most entries have links provided to connect them to an online map hosted by the National Library of Scotland, which helpfully allows you to examine the environment where your ancestors lived.

Finally for Peeblesshire, the county's most prominent heritage sites can be explored at **www.scottishbordersheritage.co.uk/49842**.

Perthshire
The Perth and Kinross Archives website (**http://tinyurl.com/ltbvod**) hosts many useful databases compiled by its Friends association. These include the *Perth Burial Registers 1794–1855*, the *Threipland's People* database (listing names of people living and working in the Threipland family estates of Perthshire and Caithness), *Women's Sources*, three separate militia-based databases and a *Perthshire People* index. Friends of the Dundee City Archives have also uploaded details of Perthshire vehicle registrations (1909–1911) at **www.fdca.org.uk/ FDCATransport1.html**. Other county wide resources for Perthshire include **www.perthshire-scotland.co.uk/towns.htm**, which hosts brief

Carr's Croft in Craigie, Perth, formerly home to a small handloom-weaving community. Author's collection

histories for main towns in the county, and the Perthshire Diary site (**www.perthshirediary.com**), which recalls 365 moments in the history of the county arranged as a daily digest.

The North Perthshire Family History Group website (**www.npfhg. org**) includes a list of the society's resources and a map of parishes covered, as well as burial and census records. The Tay Valley Family History Society (**www.tayvalleyfhs.org.uk**) carries a similar list of society holdings. The Glenlyon History Society (**www.glenlyon.org**) has several old photos and Rena Stewart's *Glenlyon Memories* recollections.

The Alternative Perth site (**www.alternative-perth.co.uk**) holds a virtual encyclopaedia of material related to the burgh of Perth (and Perthshire), with many biographies of important folk and gazetteer entries. The *Handloom Weavers of Perth* site (**www.perthweavers. bravehost.com**) names weavers found in the 1841 census for the burgh, those bearing arms in 1715, noted in rental books and charters, and paying for kirk seats in 1749. A plan of the burgh from the early 1800s is at **www.ambaile.org.uk/en/item/item_maps.jsp?item_id=18251**.

The Papers in a Trunk site at **www.highlandstrathearn.com** is another encyclopaedic project carrying essays on the history of Strathearn, with its associated clans and families. Monumental inscriptions for Little Leny in Callander are online at **www.incallander.co.uk/lit_len. htm**, whilst the names on Blairgowrie war memorial are recorded at **www.blairgowrie-sacrifice.co.uk**. Many electoral rolls for the county from 1832 can be found at **www.caledonianconnections.com**. For Blackford's history, visit **www.blackfordhistoricalsociety.org.uk**.

Dunning Parish Historical Society has a monumental inscriptions index at **www.dunning.uk.net**, and census entries from 1841–1891. Inscriptions for Dunblane are recorded at **www.memento-mori.co.uk**, with the history of the town itself recorded at **www.dunblaneweb.co.uk**.

A history of Tayside Police is found at **www.tayside.police.uk/ history.php**, whilst the earlier history of the Perthshire Volunteers is at **www.lightinfantry.org.uk/regiments/perth/perth_index.htm**.

Renfrewshire

A gazetteer description of Renfrewshire from 1847 is available at **www.myrenfrew.com/renfrew.htm**, and images from the county can be viewed at the Renfrewshire Family History Society site (**www. renfrewshirefhs.co.uk**). The Renfrewshire Local History Forum at **http://rlhf.info** promotes all aspects of history and archaeology in both

Renfrewshire and Inverclyde, whilst for information on the county's cemeteries visit **www.renfrewshire.gov.uk/ilwwcm/publishing.nsf/ Content/es-sj-cemeteries**.

A fairly comprehensive resource is the *Portal to the Past* site at **www.eastrenfrewshire.gov.uk/heritage.htm?textsize=undefined** which displays much of East Renfrewshire's heritage. It includes a detailed family history section and hosts online exhibitions such as a history of the region in the First World War, *Great Scottish Minds and Innovations*, and more focussed essays such as the history of Shanks & Co. brass foundry. The site also includes the *East Renfrewshire Heritage Database*, a catalogue of the council's archival holdings

The Greenock-based Watt Library has some useful online resources. A BMD index, as sourced from entries in local newspapers from the early nineteenth century to 1913, is available at **http://tinyurl.com/yd55wdm**, whilst a more generic newspaper archive index (subject-based) is available at **http://tinyurl.com/ydcfn5m**. The library also has an impressive photographic site at **http://tinyurl.com/ycq3h2u**.

A register of marriages and baptisms from the parish of Kilbarchan (1649–1772) is online at **www.archive.org/details/scottishrecordso41 scotuoft**, whilst some resources for Barrhead and Neilston, including census material and a forum, are available at **www.barrhead-scotland. com/Culture/history**. The history of Craigends estate is discussed at **http://craigends.net**, whilst burials for the parish of Mearns are available at **www.mearnskirkyardproject.co.uk**.

Ross and Cromarty

The *Wayfarers* site (**www.rchs.uhi.ac.uk**), from Ross and Cromarty Heritage Society, hosts various resources for many communities within the county, including war memorials, parish records and more. Ross and Cromarty Roots (**www.rosscromartyroots.co.uk**) is equally useful with contextual essays on subjects such as the Church, schools, the poor, farming and the Clearances, whilst also providing some graveyard location information. Highland Family History Society's site (**www. highlandfhs.org.uk**) includes resources for the region, whilst many of the county's folk are included in the Scottish Highlander Photo Archive (**www.scottishhighlanderphotoarchive.co.uk**).

The Am Baile website also covers the county, with one of its most impressive holdings being a 44 downloadable book on *The Cromarty Fisherfolk Dialect* at **http://tinyurl.com/y8zlxet**. For a general guide to the main towns and villages in the Black Isle visit **www.black-isle.info/ welcome.html**.

For the royal burgh of Cromarty, an 1814 militia list for males aged between 17 and 45 is at **www.cali.co.uk/users/freeway/courthouse/ geneal1.html**, whilst a list of householders from 1744 is at **www.cali. co.uk/users/freeway/courthouse/geneal2.html**.

Old photos of the region are online at **www.theoldhometown.com**, whilst a site on the history of the parish of Resolis is available at **http:// members.multimania.co.uk/ResolisBlackIsle**. A history of St Michael's Kirk near Balblair village is at **www.kirkmichael.info**.

For the Coigach in the east of the county, there are considerable resources located at **http://freepages.genealogy.rootsweb.ancestry. com/~coigach/index.htm**, including militia lists, gazetteer entries, emigration records, census records and even a 1775 map showing the locations of farms in the region.

Elsewhere in the county, an 1841 census for Urray is presented at **http://tinyurl.com/y8vm5db**, along with several returns for the Isle of Lewis (see p. X). The *Fearn Peninsula Graveyards Project* database at **www.fearnpeninsulagraveyards.com** is another excellent resource with nearly 7000 memorials. The index is free but access to the full records costs £2.50 for 24 hours.

Roxburghshire

The Borders Family History Society has a web page for Roxburghshire at **www.bordersfhs.org.uk/r_shire.asp** which includes an interactive parish map, whilst elsewhere the site also hosts a poor law records database for Jedburgh, as well as a discussion forum. The 1841–1861 censuses have been transcribed and made freely available at **www. maxwellancestry.com**, whilst several other generic websites on the Borders include material from Roxburghshire (see p. 140).

Melrose Parish Registers (1642–1840), compiled by the Scottish Record Society in 1913, can be viewed at **www.archive.org/details/ scottishrecordso33scotuoft**. For the history of Denholm, its quarrying industry, church history, stocking industry and more, see **www. denholmvillage.co.uk**.

The History of Kelso at **www.kelso.bordernet.co.uk/history** records the history of the town from 1113 to the First World War. For Maxton visit **www.maxton.bordernet.co.uk** to view the history section and some black and white images. For Jedburgh and the Borders, visit

www.jedburgh-online.org.uk for a useful history section with topics such as local ballads, and notable men and women.

Selkirkshire
Borders Family History Society (see Berwickshire) has a page for Selkirkshire at **www.bordersfhs.org.uk/s_shire.asp**, which includes a parish map. At the time of writing the page was still under construction but in due course will contain detailed listings of resources held by the society and elsewhere for the county.

The History of Selkirk site (**www.selkirk.bordernet.co.uk/history. html**) provides introductory essays on various subjects of interest, including the Covenanters, the Reivers, Selkirk Abbey and the history of the Selkirk Common Riding.

For a list of Selkirk burgh inhabitants on June sixteenth 1817 visit the Alberta Family Histories Society site at **www.afhs.ab.ca/data/ census/1817**. Selkirk Antiquarian Society's pages at **www.selkirkshire antiquariansociety.co.uk** contain lists of deaths and monumental inscriptions records which can be purchased. Transcriptions of statutory death records from the county in 1874 can also be viewed at **http:// tinyurl.com/yg2qt6b**, whilst census records from 1841–1861 are available at **www.maxwellancestry.com**.

Shetland
Shetland Museum and Archives (**www.shetlandmuseumandarchives. org.uk**) provides an online summary of local history holdings, and its fully searchable photo collection is available at **http://photos. shetland-museum.org.uk**. The islands' heritage is explored at **www. shetland-heritage.co.uk**, whilst Shetland Family History Society's site at **www.shetland-fhs.org.uk** includes a map showing various parishes across the islands.

A free database of names from across the islands, sourced from many different records, is at **www.bayanne.info/Shetland**, whilst a Shetland DNA project is hosted at **www.davidkfaux.org/shetlandislandsY-DNA**. For the 1841 and 1851 censuses for the Isle of Foula visit **http://tinyurl. om/yk7x6do** – links on the page will also take you to the 1861, 1871 and 1891 equivalents. Census returns for other Shetland districts in 1841 are available at **http://tinyurl.com/yf4sk2y**.

Janice Halcrow's *Shetland Newspaper Transactions* site at **www. jghalcrow.co.uk** lists transcripts of BMD intimations from the *Shetland*

Times from 1873 to 1900, as well as some historical news stories. Further intimations from the same paper from 1930–1988 can also be accessed at **www.users.on.net/~bruce.smith**.

Stirlingshire

Transcriptions of statutory deaths in Stirlingshire in 1869 can be found at **http://tinyurl.com/ycus7qj**, whilst many monumental indexes for burial grounds across the county can be found at **www.memento-mori. co.uk**. For the history of Stirling town, and descriptions of several heritage sites, visit **www.stirling.co.uk**.

The history of Kilsyth is explored at **www.kilsyth.org.uk**, with some monumental inscriptions for the town available at **http://members. tripod.com/~Caryl_Williams/Kilsyth-7.html**, and a handful of transcribed OPR records from 1737, 1741, 1748 and 1762 further available at **http://members.iinet.net.au/~kjstew/KilsythOPRS.htm**.

The Drymen Millenium Project (**www.drymen-history.org.uk/ millennium.html**) has a useful list of publications on Drymen's history, whilst the Milngalvie Online project (**www.milngavieonline.com**) has some history resources including a list of estates. For Killearn visit **www.killearnontheweb.co.uk**. The 1881 census for Bothkennar can be consulted freely at **http://tinyurl.com/yctb36t**.

Finally for the county, visit **www.falkirklocalhistorysociety.co.uk** for a detailed history of Falkirk.

Sutherland

The County Sutherland site (**www.countysutherland.co.uk**) contains an excellent guide to the county's communities, and includes a pay-per-view burials database, permanently accessible after a one off payment of £6. The site also has an associated blog at **http://cosuthtribute. blogspot.com** detailing those recorded on local war memorials. Sutherland is also covered by Highland Family History Society, with various resources available at its site (**www.highlandfhs.org.uk**).

The Internet Archive hosts a digitised facsimile at **www.archive. org/details/scottishrecordso26scotuoft** of a Scottish Records Society publication from 1911 containing the parish register of Durness (1764–1814).

A community site for Helmsdale at **www.helmsdale.org** includes various history essays on subjects as diverse as local football, the police, the Clearances and emigration.

West Lothian

West Lothian was known as Linlithgowshire until 1921. The council's history and heritage page (**www.westlothian.gov.uk/tourism/Local History/**) has various historical resources as well as details of the council's archival holdings. The *West Lothian Place Names Project* concerning various locations in the county and the etymology of their place names is available at **www.cyberscotia.com/west-lothian-place-names**.

West Lothian Family History Society (**www.wlfhs.org.uk**) has census indexes online for 1851 and 1901, a burial registers search facility, a parish list, a picture gallery and a History of West Lothian, whilst Lothians Family History Society's site (**www.lothiansfhs.org.uk**) hosts a public discussion forum.

For indexes to monumental inscriptions at Bo'ness, Carriden and Linlithgow visit the Memento Mori site (**www.memento-mori.co.uk**), whilst inscriptions and photos from cemeteries at Cramond, Dalmeny, Kirkliston, and South Queensferry can be viewed at **http://tinyurl.com/y9kr8us**.

A one place study for Armadale, is available at **www.armadale.org.uk/indexhistory.htm** with historic maps and more. A site on Uphall is also available at **http://uphall.org**, containing the 1841 and 1851 censuses, monumental inscriptions from St. Nicholas Kirk, war memorials, and essays on life in the village's past.

Wigtownshire

The Wigtownshire Pages at **http://freepages.history.rootsweb.ancestry.com/~leighann/index.html** include separate vital records indexes from both parish registers and the Wigtownshire Free Press (starting in 1843), a parish map, death registers transcriptions, commissariat records of Wigtown Testaments (1700–1800) and much more. The Internet Archive at **www.archive.org/details/scottishrecordso38scotuoft** hosts the Parish Lists of Wigtownshire and Minnigaff from 1684, as compiled by the Scottish Records Society in 1916.

The 1851 census for the county, and shipping registers for Wigtown (1836–1908), can be consulted at **www.dgcommunity.net/historical indexes**. The *Wigtown Cultural Heritage Project* at **www.wigtown-book town.co.uk/heritage/index.asp** also hosts a list of resources which are available on a local computer database which it states 'will eventually become available on the internet'. A 1912 trade directory for the town is available at **http://homepages.rootsweb.ancestry.com/~scottish/Trade Directory1912.html**.

Dumfries and Galloway Family History Society's website at **www. dgfhs.org.uk** has a list of parishes in the county and the years in which the surviving parish registers commenced. The website of the Stranraer and District Local History Trust at **www.stranraerhistory.org.uk** also contains lists of recordings in its audio archive and its books on the history of the county.

The Western Isles

The Western Isles never formed a single county historically, but as they formed a culturally separate community in many ways it is easier to deal with them in a single dedicated section. Within the isles are many local historical societies known as 'comainn eachdraidh' in Gaelic, and a useful gateway site for many of those based in the Outer Hebrides is An Caidreachas Eachdraidh, located at **www.ancaidreachas.com**.

Hebridean Connections (**www.hebrideanconnections.com/home. aspx**) provides various resources for the west of the Isle of Lewis,

The An Caidreachas website provides a gateway to many local historical societies. Courtesy of Sarah Egan

The ancient broch of Dun Carloway on the Isle of Lewis. Author's collection

mainly for the small island of Bernera and the districts of Uig, Pairc and Kinloch, whilst the 1841 census for Lochs, Uig, Barvas and Stornoway is at **http://tinyurl.com/y8vm5db**. Also for the west, and for St. Kilda, visit the Comann Eachdraidh an Taobh Siar site at **www.ceats.org.uk/archive.htm**.

Elsewhere on the island, for a 1718 Judicial Rental roll of Nether Barvas, a Barvas School log book from 1899 and an index to articles and photographs in *Fios a'Bhaile*, the newsletter of Comann Eachdraidh Bharabhais agus Bhru, visit **www.barvasandbrue.com**. Further resources for Ness to the north of the island are at **www.c-e-n.org**, whilst for Pairc visit **www.cepairc.com** and the Angus MacLeod Archive site at **www.angusmacleodarchive.org.uk**.

If your ancestors were from North Tosta, the local historical society's site (**www.tolsta.info**) has lists of emigrants, famous folk, galleries and a timeline. South of Lewis is Harris, and the Seallam! Visitor Centre website at **www.seallam.com** has details of holdings for the island's family history centre *Co Leis Thu?*.

For the history of Barra, Vatersay, Mingulay, Berneray, Pabbay and Sanday visit **www.barraheritage.com**. Historic images of Berneray are accessible through **www.isleofberneray.com/gallery**, whilst resources for Benbecula are available at **www.benbeculahistorysociety.co.uk**.

The holdings of the Clan Donald Centre at Armadale on Skye are explained at **www.clandonald.com**, whilst the Sleat Local History Society site at **www.sleatlocalhistorysociety.org.uk** has a Gaelic local place name index, old photographs and the histories of various townships. Inscriptions from some graves at Struan's municipal cemetery on the island are at **www.gravestonephotos.com/public/cemetery.php? cemetery=232&limit=1**. Resources for Elgol and Torrin are at the time of writing soon to go online at **www.elgolandtorrinhistoricalsociety. org.uk**.

The Isle of Eigg History Society site (**www.isleofeigg.net/heritage/ society.htm**) has some information on the island, whilst for Colonsay and Oronsay visit **www.colonsay.org.uk/Colonsay%20Records.html** to find various census extracts, gravestones inscriptions and nineteenth-century parish records. Resources for Coll can be found at **www. collgenealogy.com**, including the censuses, a map, various vital records, lists of emigrant ships and their passengers and old newspaper articles. A similar site for Tiree at **www.tireegenealogy.com** includes overseas cemetery records and material from the Napier Commission into crofting, whilst the history of Muck is explored at **www.islemuck.com/ geneal.htm**, accompanied by census transcriptions.

Mull Genealogy (**www.mullgenealogy.co.uk**) has baptism and burial indexes, and a census database for 1841, 1861, 1881 and 1901. There is also a look-ups service in the Resources section of the site for books held privately, and some further databases such as rental rolls for the Torloisk estate and deaths in Kilninian. A list of Mull natives who settled in Prince Edward Island, Canada, is online at **www.islandregister. com/mullnatives.html**. The history and genealogy of the nearby island of Lismore is explored at **www.celm.org.uk**, whilst historic images of people from the island in need of identification can be viewed at **www.isleoflismore.com**.

Pre-1875 parish, rental census and other records for the Islay are available at **http://freepages.family.rootsweb.ancestry.com/~tlarson/bdm**, whilst additional parish records for Bowmore, Killarow and Kildalton are online at **http://homepages.rootsweb.ancestry.com/~steve/islay/opr**. The Finlaggan website at **www.finlaggan.com** has the *Islay Cultural Database*, though access is by subscription. Burials at Kilearnadail graveyard are listed at **http://tinyurl.com/ylncsms**. A blog-based site for genealogy on Jura is at **www.jurainfo.com/blog/genealogy/jura-genealogy-trace-your-jura-ancestors**. For the history of Gigha and its MacNeill lairds visit **www.gigha.org.uk**.

Scottish HIghlander. Author's collection

Chapter Seven

NORTHERN IRELAND

Despite the great loss of material caused by the Irish Civil War, a great deal of genealogical material for Northern Ireland is still accessible online.

Antrim (and Belfast)
Northern Ireland's capital city of Belfast is actually included in both counties Antrim and Down, but for simplicity will be covered here. The Glenravel Local History project (**www.belfasthistoryproject.com**) has a detailed Belfast timeline from 1830s to 1941, available across several downloadable PDF files, as well as a history of Milltown cemetery, which can be purchased from the site as an e-book. For a history of Clifton Street Cemetery and a list of burials visit **www.cliftonstreet cemetery.com**. At **www.belfastfamilyhistory.com** you will find many photos of the city in the early twentieth century, rare film footage, an exhibition on Belfast and the 1911 census, and a searchable database of 60,000 people from both the 1901 and 1911 censuses, though this is predominantly for west Belfast. For east Belfast, several historic photos are available to view at **www.ebhs.org.uk**.

The Lennon Wylie site at **www.lennonwylie.co.uk** has many directories for Belfast from 1805–1910, whilst the Public Records Office website has further editions (see p. 7). Several volunteers offer directory look-ups from the twentieth century in the Belfast Forum's *Genealogy* section at **www.belfastforum.co.uk**.

The website for Queens University's Special Collections at **http:// digitalcollections.qub.ac.uk** includes a Book of Remembrance of university students and its members in the Officers' Air Training Corps

The Belfast Timeline, a collection of detailed contemporary newspaper reports from the 1830s to 1941. Courtesy of the Glenravel Local History Project

and Air Squadron from the two world wars. The Linenhall Library offers a searchable catalogue of its holdings at **www.linenhall.com**.

Away from the capital, much of the 1851 census for County Antrim has actually survived, and has been transcribed by Liam McFaul and placed online at **http://irishgenealogy.net/antrimgen.html#top**, along with material on the history of Larne.

The Glens of Antrim Historical Society has placed several articles of local interest at **www.antrimhistory.net**, as well as a video tour of the Glens and transcribed returns from projects on clachans and oral history from the area. Bill Macafee's North Antrim site (**www.billmacafee. com/index.htm**) hosts many resources including local 1766 religious census returns, the 1796 Flaxgrowers' List and more, whilst a North Antrim Local Interest List also exists in blog format at **http://nalil. blogspot.com** with much of interest for the area. The Bann Valley Genealogy Church records site includes details of many records for North Antrim at **www.torrens.org.uk/Genealogy/BannValley/church/ contents.html**.

For Ballyclare there are photo guides on local mills, history and more at **http://dnausers.d-n-a.net/UlsterHistory**, whilst Ballymoney is covered at **www.ballymoneyancestry.com**, where you will find a map of the area from 1734, a timeline, discussion of famous emigrants, a townland lists and a database of 55,000 records drawn from various sources. The United Irishmen's Battle of Antrim in 1798 is discussed at **http://tinyurl. com/yglgavo**. For my home town of Carrickfergus, where many United Irishmen were jailed, the Internet Archive offers a 1909 publication, *The History and Antiquities of the County of the Town of Carrickfergus, From the Earliest Records till 1839*, at **www.archive.org/details/historyantiquiti00 mcskiala**.

Andy Keogh's Rathlin Island website at **www.rathlin-island.info** contains a wealth of material for the island, both historical and genealogical, including the Rathlin Trees database of some 7,000 names dating back to the eighteenth century, whilst the Resources section is packed with material from the 1831 agricultural census to various lists of Rathlin folk settled in the United States. For a survey of Rathlin's clachans, visit **www.antrimhistory.net/content.php?cid=677**.

Armagh
Home to the ecclesiastical capital of Ireland for both the Anglican and Roman Catholic faiths, Armagh is superbly catered for by Dave Jassie's *County Armagh Research Material Index* at **http://freepages.genealogy. rootsweb.ancestry.com/~jassie/armagh/index-page9.html**, with many resources. The Irish Genealogy project (**www.igp-web.com/armagh/ index.htm**) includes a topographical description of the county by Samuel Lewis from 1837.

The city of Armagh's hearth tax returns from 1665 can be found at **www.failteromhat.com/armaghhearth.php**, whilst the history and heritage of Armagh Observatory is recorded at **http://star.arm.ac.uk/ history**.

The 1602 census of Fews barony is recorded at **www.mcconville.org/ main/genealogy/census1602.html**. For Armagh tales and detailed pages on the townlands of Creggan visit **www.devlin-family.com**, whilst Creggan History Society's site at **www.cregganhistory.co.uk** contains an archive with old school photos, directory entries and further townlands descriptions. Some nineteenth century baptism and marriage records for First and Second Markethill Presbyterian Church can be found at **www.markethillpresbyterian.co.uk/genealogy.htm**.

Down

Several websites offer resources at parish level for much of the county, including Ros Davies' County Down site (**http://freepages.genealogy. rootsweb.ancestry.com/~rosdavies**), Raymond's County Down site (**http:// www.raymondscountydownwebsite.com**), and the Irish Genealogy Project (**www.igp-web.com/down/index.htm**). Down County Museum's site (**www.downcountymuseum.com**) contains two convicts databases of prisoners transported to Australia, maritime photos and other resources.

For the 1901 census for the barony of Lecale, and other resources, visit **www.lecalehistory.co.uk**, whilst the 1901 and 1911 censuses for Kilkeel can be found at **http://freepages.genealogy.rootsweb.ancestry.com/ ~meaneypj**.

The Bann Valley Museum site at **www.bvph-museum.com** contains a history of Loughbrickland and Dromore, historic photos, and articles, whilst Carryduff is dealt with at **http://carryduffhistoricalsociety.org.**

Online databases for the convicts of County Down. Courtesy of County Down Museum

uk. For a 1770 map of Donaghadee and other resources visit **www. donaghadeehistoricalsociety.org.uk**, whilst Donaghmore is catered for by the Internet Archive at **www.archive.org/details/ancientirishpari 00cowarich** with the 1914 publication *An Ancient Irish Parish: Past and Present, Being the Parish of Donaghmore, County Down*. The Newry, Donaghmore, Loughbrickland and Banbridge website at **http://tinyurl. com/yfuuqe3** carries a list of landowners from 1876, and other resources, though many links are broken.

The history of Drumaroad and Clanvaraghan is detailed at **www. drumaroadhistory.com**, and Poyntpass at **www.poyntzpass.co.uk**. The Strabane History Society (**www.strabanehistorysociety.com**) discusses much of the town's past, including articles on the Volunteer Movement (1779–85) and the Strabane Corporation. Lisburn Historical Society's site (**www.lisburn.com/books/historical_society/historicalsociety.html**) carries back issues of its journal from 1978–2005/6, which can be read for free.

Fermanagh

The Irish Genealogy Project's Fermanagh pages at **www.igp-web.com/ fermanagh** contain many directories, maps, videos, estate records and more, whilst many additional resources and census substitutes can be accessed at **www.rootsweb.ancestry.com/~fianna/county/fermanagh/ fer-1.html**. The Northern Ireland Genweb page for Fermanagh is equally packed at **www.rootsweb.ancestry.com/~nirfer** with lists of settlers from the 1610 plantations, muster rolls, freeholder lists, parish records, maps, tithes applotment records and much more.

For over a thousand images of gravestones from across the county visit **www.tammymitchell.com/cofermanagh**, whilst Monaghan-based Clogher Historical Society's *Record Index* has many resources for Fermanagh also at **www.clogherhistory.ie**.

Londonderry

The Irish genealogy project pages at **www.igp-web.com/derry/ index.htm** have many resources for Derry including databases such as a Flax Growers List from 1796. The Bann Valley Genealogy Church records site includes details of many records at **www.torrens.org.uk/ Genealogy/BannValley/church/contents.html**. The Fianna County Derry site at **www.rootsweb.ancestry.com/~fianna/county/derry.html** is another useful gateway.

The Street Directories collection on the PRONI website includes holdings for Derry. By permission of the Deputy Keeper of the Records, Public Record office of Northern Ireland

George McIntyre's history of Drumlamph townland project at **http:// georgemcintyre.tripod.com** includes details on the war memorial for Castledawson, and names of many people from Bellaghy Town from 1860s-1930s. For a history of Coleraine visit **www.colerainehistorical society.org.uk**. The Public Records Office of Northern Ireland site (see p. 7) carries the *New Directory of the City of Londonderry and Coleraine, including Strabane with Lifford, Newtownlimavady, Portstewart and Portrush* in its *Street Directories* section. A blog-based resource for the history of Killowen is at **www.killowenhistory.com/wordpress**, whilst a data-base of nineteenth century Roman Catholic baptisms and marriages from Lavey is available at **www.lmi.utvinternet.com/lgyards.htm**.

Tyrone

The County Tyrone Genealogy site at **http://freepages.genealogy. rootsweb.ancestry.com/~tyrone** has a map of the county's civil parishes, many church records and Griffith's Valuation, whilst the County Tyrone

Gravestone Project (**www.tammymitchell.com/cotyrone**) has over 1100 gravestone photos from across the county. Although based just over the border, the Monaghan-based Clogher Historical Society's *Record Index* at **www.clogherhistory.ie** has many resources for Tyrone also.

The hearth tax returns for Dungannon from 1666 can be found at **http://tinyurl.com/yzjjwvv**, whilst a summary of the *Ecclesiastical Census of Clogherny* (1851–1852) can be read at **www.localpopulationstudies. org.uk/PDF/LPS29/LPS29_1982_35-49.pdf**. The history of Bready is discussed at **www.breadyancestry.com**, with the site including a townland map, and sections on Ulster Scots heritage, historical maps, and databases of 30,000 names derived from several sources.

Killeeshil and Clonaneese Historical Society has an archive with rent rolls, census returns and more at **http://killeeshilclonaneese.org/ joomla**, whilst Glenelly Historical Society (**www.glenellyhistorical. org.uk**) has essays on the Great Glenelly Flood of 1680, the Plumbridge Water Scheme and other useful local articles. For some historic images of the town of Donaghmore visit **www.donaghmorelivinghistory.com**, whilst to source the contents of past issues of Stewartstown & District Local History Society's journal *The Bell* visit **www.stewartstownhistory. co.uk**.

Chapter Eight

CROWN DEPENDENCIES

In addition to the main counties of the United Kingdom, two important island-based communities also exist in the British Isles with their own regional identities and languages. These are the Crown Dependencies of the Channel Islands, close to the Normandy Coast, and the Isle of Man, at the heart of the Irish Sea.

The Channel Islands (Les Îsles de la Manche or Les Isles Anglo-Normandes)
A series of old maps depicting the Channel Islands can be found via Genmaps at **http://tinyurl.com/ybmmok3**, whilst old postcards of Jersey, Guernsey, Alderney, Sark and Herm are accessible through a series of interactive maps at **www.cipostcard.co.nz**.

A broad history of the region is available on the *Island Life* website at **www.islandlife.org/history.htm**, with a dedicated section for each island. For general resources, Alex Glendinning's impressive and all encompassing website at **http://user.itl.net/~glen/CIintro.html** is the regional equivalent of GENUKI and is packed with useful links. Births and baptisms (1820–1907) are hosted at FamilySearch's Record Search pilot.

The Isle of Man (Ellan Vannin)
Information about civil registration, probate and land registration for Man is available from the Manx Government at **www.gov.im/registries**. For heritage issues, visit the Manx National Heritage site at **www.gov.im/mnh**.

Useful genealogical resources are listed at **www.ukisearch.com/ isleofman.html**, whilst discussion forums are hosted by the Isle of Man Family History Society at **www.iomfhs.im**, with the site also carrying a photo gallery of images from across the island. A map of Man's seventeen parishes is online at **www.isleofman.com/heritage/genealogy/ genealogy.aspx**, along with other resources such as a look-up exchange, message boards and some family GEDCOM files. The FamilySearch Record Search pilot site hosts baptisms from 1821–1911 and marriages from 1841–1911.

Manorial rent rolls from 1540 for several parishes can be found at **www.manxroots.info**, whilst Frances Coakley's A Manx Note Book site (**www.isle-of-man.com/manxnotebook**) hosts a packed compendium of essays and resources relating to the island.

Chapter Nine

EMPIRE AND MIGRATION

As an island, Britain has seen its fair share of migrants coming and going across the centuries, and this chapter examines many of the records that can help to trace their progress.

Immigration

One of the best websites for dealing with the subject of migration into Britain is Moving Here (**www.movinghere.org.uk**), with many resources on the history from the last two centuries of people arriving from the Caribbean and South Asia, as well as the Irish and Jews. Not only does the site host timelines and topical essays concerning the history of each group, it also provides handy family history research guides covering a range of subjects. It also hosts many genealogical resources, such as digitised images of crew lists for vessels sailing from Calcutta to London in the 1820s, photographs of Jewish children arriving in Britain on the kindertransport, and maps of old Irish poor law unions.

Stories of persecution feature heavily amongst groups who have settled in Britain, and many have sought to preserve their histories on-line. French protestant Huguenots were one such group who started to settle in Britain in the late seventeenth century, and there are several resources that can help to establish your Huguenot ancestry. These include the website of the Huguenot Society of Great Britain and Ireland (**www.huguenotsociety.org.uk**) and the Huguenot Surnames Index (**www.aftc.com.au/Huguenot/hug.html**), which allows you to contact other families with proven lineages back to France.

The Moving Here website. Courtesy of The National Archives

A useful resource for children who fled Nazi Germany, Austria, Poland and Czechoslovakia on the kindertransports between December 1938 and the start of the Second World War, is the Kindertransport Association site (**www.kindertransport.org**). For resources on Jewish immigration to Britain you should consult the JewishGEN website (**www.jewishgen.org.uk**), the Jewish Genealogical Society of Great Britain (**www.jgsgb.org.uk**), and the Scottish Jewish Archive Centre (**www.sjac.org.uk**).

A key problem for many is to work out exactly from where our ancestors first originated. The census records from 1841–1911 can be useful in identifying a country of origin (more specifically from 1851 onwards), but it is worth noting that countries as identified today may not be the same as recorded 150 years ago – for example, a person noted as being from 'Russia' may in fact be from what is now called Poland. Naturalisation papers may also help, and TNA has a helpful guide on such records at **www.nationalarchives.gov.uk/catalogue/ RdLeaflet.asp?sLeafletID=243**. The *England, Alien Arrivals 1810–1811,*

1826–1869 collection on Ancestry is sourced from many lists compiled by the Home Office, Foreign Office and Customs records as held at TNA (FO 83/21-22, HO 2, HO 3, CUST 102/393-396), and names many settlers arriving in Britain.

Records of an immigrant ancestor's original voyage to the UK can also provide further clues. Ancestry's *UK Incoming Passenger Lists 1872–1960* database contains passenger records held by TNA as part of its Board of Trade records series (BT 26), but does not list voyages from Europe or the Mediterranean, and is incomplete prior to 1890. Where an entry can be found, however, the original manifest can be viewed, providing information such as names, ages, occupations, ports and dates of departure and arrival, vessel name and the shipping line, not to mention the details of other members of the family who may have travelled with your ancestor.

As various migrant groups arrived and settled in Britain, they established their own churches and kept their own registers. Many records for Russian Orthodox, French, Dutch, Swiss and German congregations which settled in London will be found in the non-conformist record collections at the Genealogist website or at **www. bmdregisters.co.uk.**

The Port Cities website at **www.portcities.org.uk** provides a great deal of information on the maritime history of Bristol, Hartlepool, Liverpool, London and Southampton, and has a great deal of material on the lives of workers from ethnic communities who worked in these ports, as well as a substantial section on the history of slavery within the pages for Bristol.

For the most ethnically diverse part of the country, the Untold London website (**www.untoldlondon.org.uk**) provides a great deal of information on the various communities to have settled in the capital with links to many exciting projects such as that recording recent Kurdish history in London, the community having arrived en masse some twenty years ago, and today believed to number over 50,000 people. A similar site exists for Bristol at **www.englandspastforeveryone. org.uk/Counties/Bristol/Projects/EthnicMinorities**, covering the history of the Irish, Welsh, Jewish, African, Asians and Polish settlers. In Scotland, a useful site for the Italian migrants who settled is the Scots Italian project at **www.scotsitalian. com.**

If your ancestor is from an African or Caribbean background it is worth consulting TNA's online exhibition entitled *Black Presence: Asian and Black History in Britain 1500–1850* at **www.nationalarchives.gov.**

uk/pathways/blackhistory. The Caribbean Surname Index is another worthwhile site at **www.candoo.com/surnames**, which is a discussion forum-based facility that can allow you to share material with others who may be familiar with your particular ancestor. For Birmingham, a useful site on black history can be found at **www.birminghamblack history.com**, whilst a similar site for Bright and Hove's Asian and black communities is **www.black-history.org.uk**. The CASBAH website (**www. casbah.ac.uk**) provides a portal to many links for those researching Caribbean, Black and Asian peoples in the UK.

Emigration
The British Empire was first founded in the latter sixteenth century and reached its zenith towards the end of the nineteenth century, before ending in the mid twentieth century. Channel 4's *Empire's Children* website, located at **http://channel4.empireschildren.co.uk**, provides histories of each country and guides on how to research records within them. The Royal Commonwealth Society has a massive library of resources for both the Empire and the Commonwealth, and its online catalogue at **www.lib.cam.ac.uk/deptserv/rcs** also has details of over 300,000 holdings, including books, pamphlets, periodicals, official publications, manuscripts and photographs. TNA further provides a detailed guide to the empire at **www.nationalarchives.gov.uk/education/empire-industry.htm**. For the later period into the twentieth century, the outward bound passenger manifests of journeys made from Britain and Ireland between 1890 and 1960 can be found at both **www.ancestor sonboard.com** and FindmyPast, recording some 24 million passengers from TNA's BT 27 series.

The following sections detail some of the resources from overseas countries which may also help with your research.

Canada
The Library and Archives Canada site (**www.collectionscanada.gc.ca**) contains many wonderful resources and indexes, such as the censuses, records for the military and migration to the country, and various online guides to help with your Canadian research. Ancestry also has many migration and naturalisation records, accessible through a worldwide subscription. FamilySearch hosts births (1661–1959), marriages (1661–1949), and deaths/burials (1664–1955), as well as the 1851, 1871 and 1891 censuses.

For Ontario, the Upper Canada Genealogy site at **www.uppercanada genealogy.com** includes indexes to many records collections, whilst the Archives of Manitoba site at **www.gov.mb.ca/chc/archives** has several guides and catalogues including information on how to access the Hudson's Bay Company Archive. The Newfoundland's Grand Banks project at **http://ngb.chebucto.org** hosts many historic articles, passenger lists, directories, vital records, censuses, parish records and more.

Canadian Passenger Lists from 1865–1935 and Form 30A Ocean Arrivals immigration forms from 1919–24 can be found at Ancestry via its worldwide subscription package. Additional Canadian passenger lists can also be found at the Ships Lists site (**www.theshipslist.com**), which also covers the USA, Australia and South Africa.

USA

A general gateway site for United States resources is the US GenWeb site at **www.rootsweb.ancestry.com/usgenweb**. The Library of Congress Online Catalog at **http://catalog.loc.gov** can help to source many American publications, photos and media of interest, whilst the National Archives site at **www.archives.gov** has a great deal of guides and resources on its site for genealogical research. For a list of state archives, visit **www.archives.gov/research/alic/reference/state-archives.html**, whilst a guide to state historical societies is found at **www.stenseth. org/us/statehs.html**.

The United States is of course a country that thrived on immigration, and a great deal of material is available to help you pursue your ancestors' journeys to a new life. From 1892 to 1954, the federal immigration centre at Ellis Island was the main port of entry, and digitised passenger lists for all vessels which docked there can be viewed at **www.ellisisland.org**. Prior to 1892, many who came to the States passed through Castle Garden, the nation's first official immigration centre. From 1820–1892 some 11 million immigrants went through its doors, and their details can be found at **www.castlegarden.org**. Further migration resources including a database of Irish immigrants who arrived from 1846–51 during the famine, naturalisation records, federal and state census records and more can be found at Ancestry, via its world subscription package.

For earlier settlers, the Virtual Jamestown project (**www.virtualjames town.org**), commemorating America's first British colony in Virginia has many databases such as lists of those present on indentures, court records and more, whilst Price and Associates' Immigrant Servants database (**www.immigrantservants.com**) lists over 20,000 indentures for servants, redemptioners, and transported convicts between 1607 and 1820. For a database of Welsh Mormon immigrants, and additional resources on their emigration and settlement, visit **http://welshmormon history.org**.

Many historic American newspapers have been digitised and made available online, with both Google News and WorldVitalRecords containing substantial collections.

Jamaica and the Caribbean

The Registrar General of Jamaica's site at **www.rgd.gov.jm** has information on how to apply for vital records, whilst the Jamaica Archives and Records Department has an online presence at **www.jard.gov.jm**. For the British Library's guide to Caribbean holdings, visit **www.bl.uk/ reshelp/findhelpregion/americas/caribbean**.

The National Library of Jamaica has many digitised collections online at **www.nlj.gov.jm** including *A Commemoration of the Abolition of the Slave Trade in the West Indies* bibliography and *Jamaica Unshackled*, containing digitised documents and images for the 1831 Sam Sharpe rebellion, the 1865 Morant Bay Rebellion and the 1938 Labour Riots. FamilySearch hosts Jamaican births and baptisms from 1752–1920, whilst for the Caribbean in general it has births (1590–1928), marriages (1591–1905 and deaths (1790–1906).

The National Archive's Guy Grannum has created a useful section on the Moving Here website for tracing Caribbean ancestors at **www. movinghere.org.uk/galleries/roots/caribbean/caribbean.htm**. A guide to various holdings of archives in the Caribbean is provided at **www. heritagedocs.org**. Further gateway sites for Caribbean resources include Caribbean Roots (**www.caribbeanroots.co.uk**), the Caribbean Genweb Project (**www.rootsweb.ancestry.com/~caribgw**) and the Caribbean Genealogy Research site at **www.candoo.com/genresources**.

South America

The British Settlers in Argentina and Uruguay site at **www.argbrit.org** has many records online including baptisms, marriages, deaths and burials from the Anglican and Scots Presbyterian churches, transcripts from the National Archives in Buenos Aires and London, and returns from the Argentinean censuses.

For the story of the Welsh in Patagonia, Argentina, visit both **www. welsh-patagonia.com** and the excellent Glaniad website at **www.glaniad.**

com, whilst for Scots in Patagonia visit **http://myweb.tiscali.co.uk/scots inargpat**.

Australia

The National Archives of Australia (**www.naa.gov.au**) site has various resources and guides to family history including a name search feature that allows you to search for records of immigration. The National Library of Australia site (**www.nla.gov.au/oz/genelist.html**) hosts a detailed web guide for all Australian state libraries and archives, as well as vital records access, cemeteries databases, convicts databases, military service, and other useful repositories. The library's impressive *Trove* facility (**http://trove.nla.gov.au**) is also well worth searching, containing millions of digitised records. The Australian Family History compendium site at **www.cohsoft.com.au/afhc** has similar details for useful institutions, whilst the Australian Dictionary of National Biography can be consulted at **http://adbonline.anu.edu.au**.

The Sydney-based Society of Australian Genealogists (**www.sag. org.au**) has various online research guides covering everything from adoptions in New South Wales to Ships and Voyages. Convict ancestors tend to be a badge of honour Down Under these days and the Convicts to Australia site (**www.convictcentral.com**) provides a guide to researching your ancestral felons. The National Library of Australia's Australian Newspapers collection at **http://newspapers.nla.gov.au/ndp/del/home** has many free to access digitised titles for the continent from 1803–1954. The Ryerson Index (**www.ryersonindex.org**) has a database of almost two and a half million death notices as extracted from contemporary newspapers.

New Zealand

The New Zealand Society of Genealogists site at **www.genealogy. org.nz** contains a Shipping Database from 1840–1975 and a First Families Index which can help you to pursue the earliest migrants to the country. Pearl's Pad (**http://pearlspad.net.nz**) equally has many historical resources for tracing migration.

The New Zealand Government has a Births, Deaths and Marriages Online site at **www.bdmonline.dia.govt.nz** which provides indexes for historical vital events, namely births prior to 100 years ago, marriages prior to 80 and deaths prior to 50 years (or at least for those with a date of birth at last 80 years ago).

Archives New Zealand has a catalogue on its site at **www.archway. archives.govt.nz** and includes access to details of New Zealand Defence Force records, some of which are digitised. The New Zealand History Online site at **www.nzhistory.net.nz** includes a war memorials register with some 450 sites listed

Other resources to help you trace your New Zealand kin include the papers past website (**http://paperspast.natlib.govt.nz/cgi-bin/papers past**) with digitised copies of 58 newspaper titles from 1839–1932, whilst Victoria University's New Zealand Electronic Text Centre at **www. nzetc.org** has many transcribed entries from books and other resources. For the Dictionary of New Zealand Biography, with some 3000 biographical entries, visit **www.dnzb.govt.nz**. The Otago Settlers Museum website at **www.otago.settlers.museum** hosts guides to both shipping lists and genealogical resources held within its archive. Further resources for Otago and the Southlands can be explored through guides at **www. library.otago.ac.nz/hocken/genealogists.html**.

South Africa

The South African National Archives and Records Service has many online databases at **www.national.archives.gov.za** for gravestones, heraldry, documentary archives, audio visual material and more. For early British migrants the British 1820 Settlers to South Africa site (**www.1820settlers.com**) carries many compiled genealogies, ships lists and other resources, whilst the South African genealogy site (**www. sagenealogy.co.za**) includes a data archive with passenger lists and wrecks survivors, and operates a useful blog at **www.southafrican genealogy.blogspot.com**. The Ancestry 24 site (**http://ancestry24.com**) has many free databases, such as an index to *British Residents at the Cape 1795–1819*, civil service lists, burials records, slaves deaths notices and church records.

India

The first port of call for Indian research is the Families in British India Society site at **www.fibis.org**, which includes listings from cemeteries, directories, military records, photographs, publications, schools, probate indexes, vital and parish records and more. The British Library's India Office Family History Search index at **http://indiafamily.bl.uk/UI** also lists some 300,000 vital records. For burials in India there are two useful projects, the British burials in India site at **www.indian-cemeteries.org**, and the British Association for Cemeteries in South Asia site at **www.**

bacsa.org.uk, which carries an index to cemetery inscriptions in areas previously occupied by the East India Company; also worth consulting for East India Company ancestry is **www.honeastindiaco.com**. Almost 300 films depicting life in the final years of the British Raj in India have been placed online by the Centre for South Asian Studies at Cambridge University at **www.s-asian.cam.ac.uk/archome.html**.

The Digital Library of India (**www.new.dli.ernet.in**) has transcribed texts from several publications including many on British subjects in India, whilst the *Indiaman* magazine can be subscribed to online at **www.indiaman.com**. For Anglo-Indian connections visit **www.anglo-indians.com** to find a database of *Famous Anglos* and a detailed history.

The Moving Here website also hosts a guide at **www.movinghere.org.uk/galleries/roots/asian/asian.htm**, written by Abi Husaini, for tracing ancestors in the south of Asia. For ancestors in Sri Lanka, the International Ceylon database (**www.ceylondatabase.net/Genealogy.html**) may help.

Gibraltar

For the gateway to the Mediterranean, Gibraltar Genealogy (**www.gibraltargenealogy.com**) is a useful first port of call, whilst the British Library has information on its Gibraltar Collections at **www.bl.uk/reshelp/findhelpregion/europe/gibraltar/gibraltarcoll/gibcol.html**.

The FamilySearch site also hosts birth records from 1704–1876 and marriages from 1879–1918.

Chapter Ten

SOCIAL NETWORKING

Throughout this book I have looked at many websites which offer digitised or indexed resources, historic context and handy to use research guides, but an increasingly useful facility offered by the internet is social networking. Using the web we can collaborate in constructing family trees with relatives, create life-based archive projects, and communicate in a variety of forms. We can even create websites and use our already accumulated information as a way to attract others towards our research, or study online family history courses from home, such as those offered by Pharos Teaching and Tutoring Ltd (**www.pharostutors.com**).

Sharing Data
Most of the commercial record vendors offer family tree building programmes on their sites, such as Ancestry, FindmyPast and the Genealogist, usually for free, with which you can integrate findings from their collections.

Tribal Pages (**www.tribalpages.com**) and Geni (**www.geni.com**) are two sites where you can freely create a tree from scratch online. Using these you can also search in other people's trees for possible connections, and contact them if you find a match through an internal e-mail system for members. GenesReunited works in a similar manner, but has additional resources online (see p. 13).

The MyHeritage site (**www.myheritage.com**) has a tree building and social networking facility through which you can upload photos which the site can recognise and organise through facial tagging software. It also allows you to download a copy of its *Family Tree Builder* software, probably the best downloadable free software around at present.

Increasingly, sites with a few more bells and whistles are making their way online. Arcalife (**www.arcalife.com**) allows you to build a tree, but also to create an entire life-based archive, preserving your story in a variety of ways from 'life cubes' to web-based 'time capsules', where you can also upload videos, photos, and much more. The basic subscription is free, but there are also premium-based and lifetime-based accounts which add more storage and other features.

Located at **http://familyhistory.hhs.gov**, the US-based My Family Health Portrait site encourages people to create a form of family tree diagram known as a 'genogram', used by many within the medical profession, which specifically illustrates your family health history.

Other networks
Using a family tree to form the basis of a social network is one way to share information, but it is by no means the only method. Ancestral Atlas (**www.ancestralatlas.com**), for example, uses a map as its starting point. The service allows you to tag a location with a note concerning a

Ancestral Atlas uses a map as a basis to search for genealogical links in a community. Image Copyright Ancestral Atlas Ltd

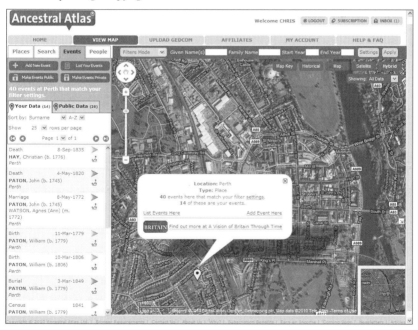

historic event that took place there, and to view the tags placed by others in the same area. If a vital event of interest, for example is noted on a tag on the same street where your ancestor lived, you could contact the person who placed it online for further information. The site also has additional features such as access to historic maps for the same area in question, and is subscription-based, with the most basic level being free to access.

Sticking on the geographic theme, Curious Fox (**www.curiousfox. com**) foregoes the maps as a connecting route, and instead forges connections by village or town names, allowing you to look-up a place and to see if there are any posts for that location which tie in to your research. Lost Cousins (**www.lostcousins.com**) is another site which allows you to form connections, in this case with the descendants of people named in census entries that you submit to the site, so long as they too are registered and have entered the same details. The censuses it bases its network on include 1841 and 1881 for England and Wales, 1881 for Scotland and 1911 for Ireland.

Chat

Discussion forums can be of immense help for your research. Rootschat (**www.rootschat.com**), British Genealogy (**www.british-genealogy.com**), Talking Scot (**www.talkingscot.com**) and ScotFamTree (**http://scot famtree.11.forumer.com**) are just some of the many independent sites that provide thread-based discussion on a country, county or subject defined basis. Some genealogy magazines provide forums, such as *Your Family Tree* (**www.yourfamilytreemag.co.uk/yft-forum**) and ABM Publishing's *Practical Family History* and *Family Tree* magazines (**www. familyhistoryforum.co.uk**), which provides for a degree of interactivity between the readers, but also the editorial teams. Ancestry also provides the excellent Rootsweb site (**www.rootsweb.ancestry.com**) which hosts message boards and mailing lists which work in a similar way.

Genealogy Wise (**www.genealogywise.com**) hosts many dedicated research groups for names, or territories or interests, chat rooms and discussion forums, blogs, a video room and more, whilst dedicated social networking sites such as Facebook (**www.facebook.com**) are increasingly hosting specific community sites for genealogy enthusiasts.

Interactive archives are also on the increase, with sites such as StoryVault (**www.storyvault.com**) hosting an archive of stories submitted by people from all over the world, in video or text format, with an online family tree capability. On a personal level, obituary sites such as Everlasting (**www.everlasting.uk.com**) allow you to leave a final tribute to a loved one, or to construct an archive of tributes, which can remain hosted online and even be printed off in book format as a more permanent lasting tribute.

Blogs
The weblog or 'blog' is another increasingly useful way to share news or research, allowing you to post updates in a diary format on a regular basis.

Many sites offer the ability to create a blog for free, such as Blogger (**www.blogger.com**) and WordPress (**http://wordpress.org**), and there are many dedicated genealogy blogs around to keep you aware of developments in the big wide family history world. My own Scottish GENES (GEnealogy News and EventS) blog at (**www.scottishancestry.blogspot. com**), for example, is built using Blogger, Alan Stewart's excellent Grow Your Own Family Tree news blog (**http://growyourownfamilytree. wordpress.com**) employs WordPress, whilst Dick Eastman's Online Genealogy Newsletter (**http://blog.eogn.com**) provides an American perspective on many British and Irish events. Useful directory site providing links to many genealogy blogs include Alltop (**http://genealogy. alltop.com**) and Geneabloggers (**www.geneabloggers.com**).

Genealogy vendors are also beginning to use blogs more to communicate their latest developments, such as FindmyPast (**http://blog. findmypast.co.uk**) and Ancestry (**http://blogs.ancestry.com/uk**). Blogs can also be employed to provide tips, such as the MacGenealogist site (**http://macgenealogist.com**) offering regular tips for Mac users.

Twitter
The free to access Twitter site (**http://twitter.com**) allows people to leave short status messages, or 'tweets', of up to 140 characters in length only, providing for a quick update on the status of those you may wish to follow, perhaps a historian or genealogical records supplier. In many cases posters will give a quick message and provide a link to a website to follow up the story discussed, making it an effective way to stay on top of developments.

You can follow people anonymously – for example, for news of further offerings from Pen and Sword you can follow **@penswordbooks**, and for yours truly **@chrismpaton** – and block those you do not wish to follow you.

FURTHER READING

BIGWOOD, Rosemary (2006) *The Scottish Family Tree Detective*. Manchester, Manchester University Press

FOWLER, Simon (2006) *Tracing Your Army Ancestors*. Barnsley, Pen and Sword Books Ltd

FOX-DAVIES, Arthur (1978) *A Complete Guide to Heraldry*. New York, Bonanza Books

GRANUM, Karen, & TAYLOR, Nigel (2004) *Wills and Other Probate Records*. London, The National Archives

GRENHAM, John (2006) *Tracing Your Irish Ancestors*. Dublin, Gill and MacMillan Ltd

HERBER, Mark (2005) *Ancestral Trails*. Sparkford, Sutton Publishing Ltd

HEY, David (2010) *The Oxford Companion to Family and Local History*. Oxford, Oxford University Press

HIGGS, Edward (2005) *Making Sense of the Census Revisited*. London, Institute of Historical Research/National Archives

KURZWEIL, Arthur (2004) *From Generation to Generation: How to Trace Your Jewish Genealogy and Family History*. San Francisco, Jossey-Bass

MASTERS, Charles (2009) *Essential Maps for Family Historians*. Newbury, Countryside Books

MAXWELL, Ian (2010) *Tracing Your Northern Irish Ancestors*. Barnsley, Pen and Sword Books Ltd

NAS (2009), *Tracing Your Scottish Ancestors – The Official Guide (5th ed.)*. Edinburgh, Birlinn Ltd

PATON, Chris (2010) *Researching Scottish Family History*. Bury, Family History Partnership

POMEROY, Chris (2007) *Family History in the Genes*. London, The National Archives

TATE, W.E. (1983) *The Parish Chest*. Chichester, Phillimore & Co. Ltd

WATERS, Colin (2009) *Family History on the Net: New Edition 2009–10*. Newbury, Countryside Books

INDEX